This volume of photographs reflects the YMCA's proud heritage in a way words seldom can. Writers struggle to catch the essence of the major motives of our lives: love, honor, pity, compassion, sacrifice, hope. But the camera can find them all, can hold them fast for generations. In the old faces and the new we can measure ourselves, sometimes smile, and take inspiration to move ahead.

We were pleased to lend a hand to this project and are proud to be associated with a great American institution—the Young Men's Christian Association.

Alexander & Alexander is an international insurance brokerage, risk management and employee benefits consulting firm serving the needs of business and individuals worldwide.

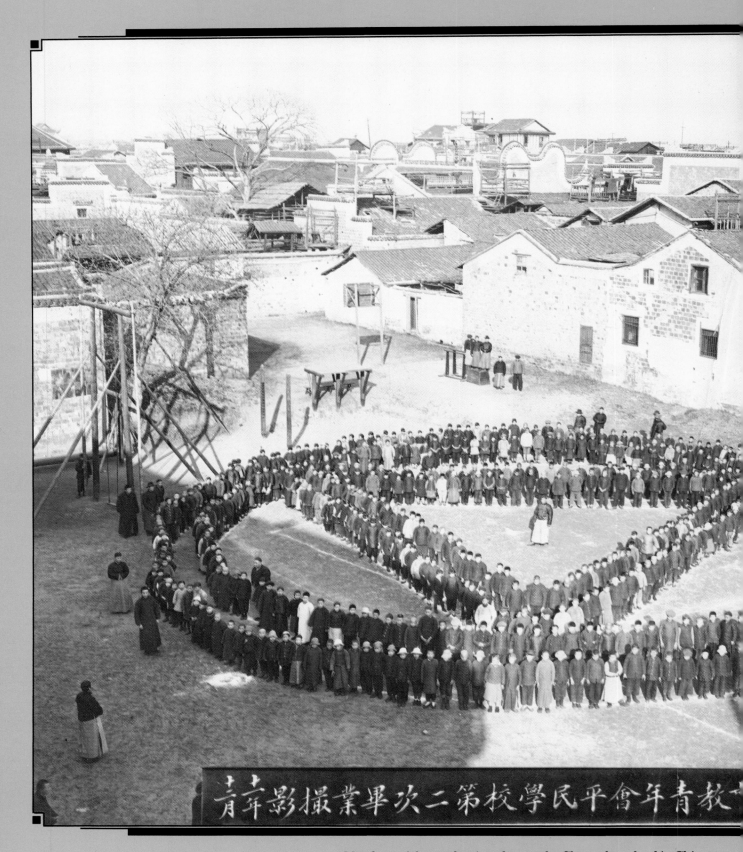

青年影撮業畢次二第校學民平會年青教十

Members of the graduating class at the Changsha school in China

PROUD HERITAGE

A History in Pictures of the YMCA in the United States

Andrea Hinding

THE
DONNING COMPANY
PUBLISHERS
NORFOLK/VIRGINIA BEACH

Friends at the Hooker Outdoor Center of the YMCA of Greater New Haven, Connecticut, 1985.

Prize-winning float entered by the YMCA day care center in the annual Moultrie, Georgia, Christmas parade, 1985.

Copyright © 1988 by The National Council of Young Men's Christian Associations of the United States of America

The Donning Company/Publishers
5659 Virginia Beach Boulevard
Norfolk, Virginia 23502

Design by Sharon Varner Moyer

Edited by Liliane McCarthy
Richard A. Horwege, Senior Editor

Library of Congress Cataloging-in-Publication Data:

Hinding, Andrea.
  Proud heritage: a history in pictures of the YMCA in the United States/by Andrea Hinding.
    p.   cm.
  ISBN 0-89865-637-0 (lim. ed.)
  1. YMCA of the USA—History.   2. YMCA of the USA—History—Pictorial works. I. Title.
BV1040.H56   1988
267'.39730'222—dc19   88-5102
                                                            CIP

Printed in the United States of America

*For
Jacob Bowne, the first keeper
of the YMCA record*

*and for
David Holst, who cares about history
and laughs in all the right places*

Getting directions at the Camp Speers-
Eljabar YMCA, Dingmans Ferry,
Pennsylvania.

Contents

Preface

This is a history, in pictures, of the Young Men's Christian Association in the United States. The photographs here tell us a wonderful story of how people help and care for each other and of how our ways of serving and expressing Christian concern change over time. Like all human stories, this one has its comic moments—and its foibles and failures as well. It is a graphic record of the proud tradition in which today's YMCA members stand.

Acknowledgments

The YMCA is blessed with many friends of its history and its archives. Chief among them today are Solon Cousins and Bob Goff, who stand in the tradition of the earliest executive guardians of the record. Their determination to make the archives of the YMCA of the USA, which are now deposited at the University of Minnesota, available for widest possible use made this history possible.

Many in the YMCA community have shared their ideas, memories, and understanding of the YMCA with me. I am deeply grateful to Max Clowers, Jean Burkhardt, Harry Brunger, Gene Shaffer, Jim Gilbert, Ellie Murphy, and John O'Melia, who are poets and philosophers, one and all. Harry McCarty flew to Chicago one morning to bring back a suitcase full of railroad records, and Doug Bailey drove a truck full of Armed Services records to Minnesota. Augie Becker, Hal Gibbs, Herb Johnson, and many other members of the old guard offered their stories and their documents—and their abiding commitment to the history and future of the YMCA.

Don Kent called me to make sure that I had noticed the photograph of the divers who now grace the dust cover of this book. Bob Masuda defined fellowship as the joy of inclusion and so titled the last chapter. One hundred thirty-seven member associations contributed contemporary photographs for the project.

I am also grateful to archivist colleagues who provided information from their holdings: Shonnie Finnegan, Tom Hickerson, and Mary Bell. Mary Hedge shared the treasures of the archives of the YMCA of Metropolitan New York. Susan Grigg knew, as always, where I should begin. Alice Wilcox found the answers.

The current health of the archives owes much to financial support from the YMCA of the USA and from the National Endowment for the Humanities, which gave the University of Minnesota a grant to arrange and describe the collection. The university itself has been a generous supporter of archives in general and of this collection in particular. Frank Immler and Joseph Branin join a long list of administrators and scholars to whom the users of records owe a debt. We are grateful to the YMCA of the USA Archives Committee, chaired by Ernie Chapman, for its support.

The current health of the archives also owes much to its staff. Kendal Lyon rescued 10,000 photographs and made them available for research; her assistance, which has been both skilled and caring, was critical for this project. Dagmar Getz brought her professional competence and remarkable knowledge of foreign work and world service to this history. Dave Carmichael scoured his hundreds of boxes to fill in numerous blanks. In all things, Dave Klaassen helps. So, too, do our talented, irreverent student assistants: Joyce Forsgren, Toni Nelson, Gamila Zelada, Jill Jacobson, and Dan Sutherland.

Not least, I am grateful to the staff of Marketing and Communications of the YMCA of the USA—to Jan McCormick, who makes things happen; to Laura DesEnfants, who suggested the use of vignettes and gave the author design advice; to Charles Firke for his skill with words and his comprehensive intelligence; and to Tony Ripley, who envisioned the form this history would take and then quoted Learned Hand and Satchel Paige to help me finish.

—Andrea Hinding
January 11, 1988

A Note to Readers

Language use changes over 144 years. The YMCA is that old, and many words and titles have shifted meaning or have been purposely altered along the way. To preserve the historical flavor of this book, the author has used the language of the times where possible, rather than translate it into modern idiom.

In some cases where meaning is unclear, it is explained in brackets. In others, the old words stand. Thus "colored work," as it was called, has not been changed to "serving blacks" while "conserves" is explained.

Volunteer leaders were known to an earlier age as lay leaders. Professional staff members were called employed officers. Today's Ys are staffed by directors, once called secretaries. The top staff person at a YMCA today is usually referred to as the executive director or president or general executive instead of the old title of executive secretary or general secretary.

The national office itself has gone through several name changes:

1854-61   Central Committee of the Confederation of YMCAs of the U.S. and British Provinces

1864-79   Executive Committee of the Convention of YMCAs of the U.S. and British Provinces

1879-1924 International Committee of YMCAs of the U.S.A. and Canada

1924-81   National Board of YMCAs

1981-   YMCA of the USA.

If this volume should warm a reader's interest in a more thorough examination of YMCA history, a reading list is available. Write the YMCA Archives, 2642 University Avenue, St. Paul, Minnesota 55114.

Introduction

It is close to impossible to define the YMCA with precision because of its sprawling, inclusive, and innovative nature. We try to write it all down and the list grows so bulky that definition loses all boundaries and fails to define. We end up always with *et cetera*.

The Y is swimming lessons, the people's health club, summer camp, Leaders Club, job training, Hi-Y, child care, aerobics, emergency relief, youth sports, infant-parent classes, day camp, teen dances, family activities, international events, tutoring, adult leagues, self-improvement groups, racquetball, shelters, basketball, trips and outings, gymnastics, residential rooms, Youth and Government, aquatic exercise, programs for seniors, Indian Guide programs, community development, outdoor education, support of Ys overseas, softball and baseball, English as a second language classes, strength training, preschool aquatics, art programs, etc., stretching as far as community need and imagination can pull it.

Part of the reason the Y has lasted for so many years is that it never really narrowed its focus to serve a limited group—only boys, or only those with a certain medical problem, or only those from a single economic class. It stayed flexible, pitching in where help was needed.

That flexibility is maintained today. Ys are not a franchise in which all must cook the french fries just so and mix the special sauce precisely. Instead they are independently operated with loose strings to each other.

A major contribution that Andrea Hinding makes in her sensitive work on this book is avoiding the duke's mixture of programming on the endless list above and, instead, putting before our eyes the sharp contrasts between today and yesterday in this ever-changing organization.

She starts us with the YMCA when it was exclusively Protestant and male and moves us through the years. Today the constituents have changed but the values remain the same. It is family focused, offers hundreds of community services, and opens its doors and its board rooms to all faiths and all men and women.

The changes have not come with ease. She shows them to us in pictures and bits of searing text. But this book is not a reader. It is a looker.

The YMCA that emerges from these pages is about people. Its mission drives it to mold the kind of people who care about each other, who are firm in their sense of worth, who truly believe that everyone is a child of God and worthy of respect, who try to control the events of their own lives rather than passively waiting for events to assume control, and who give leadership to others.

YMCAs in 90 countries around the globe constitute a force working for good will, for relief of human suffering, for renewal, for reversing moral disintegration. In short, Ys are a force for hope.

—Anthony Ripley
Editor
Discovery YMCA

The 1919 champions at a California YMCA.

YMCA Mission

*The YMCA is a charitable association dedicated
to building healthy spirit, mind, and body.
Part of a worldwide movement, it puts Christian principles
into practice through programs that promote
good health, strong families, youth leadership,
community development, and international understanding.
YMCAs are open to men, women, and children
of all ages, incomes, abilities, races, and religions
at over 2,000 locations in 50 states.*

Sir George Williams, the founder of the Young Men's Christian Association in London, as an artist imagined he looked in 1844 and as the mature leader of the YMCA.

Chapter 1

A New Product of the Gospel

When George Williams and 11 other young clerks formed the first Young Men's Christian Association in London in June 1844, they began a world movement. But Williams and his friends were unaware of the significance of their act. On that day, meeting in a room in the dry goods firm of Hitchcock and Rogers, where most of them worked and lived, they were concerned simply with helping young men like themselves find God.

London in the mid-nineteenth century was indeed a place to imperil souls. Tens of thousands of young men had migrated there from the countryside to find employment. They worked 12 or 14 hours each day, and in dry goods firms most lived crowded together in small rooms above the shops. For six days each week, most of them "could only go from their beds to the counter, and from the counter to their beds." On the seventh day, some attended religious services. Most went to taverns or brothels—any place that was warm, cheerful, and well lighted.

Williams and his friends had, in John Wesley's words, felt their souls strangely warmed by God. The dangers of "vice" troubled them, but their purpose in organizing was not negative. They wanted to extend God's grace to unconverted young men so they could "feel the warmth and glow that is ours."

In the United States, Thomas Valentine Sullivan, a retired sea captain and lay missionary for the Baptist Church, also worried about the temptations facing young men in large cities. In October 1851, he read an account of the London association in the Boston *Watchman and Reflector*. He visited the London association and then returned to Boston to convene a meeting, on December 15, to discuss forming an association in that city. He and six others drafted a constitution that was reviewed at a second meeting a week later. On December 29, in the chapel of the Old South Church in Spring Lane, they approved the constitution and began their work to improve "the spiritual and mental condition of young men."

The chapel of the Old South Church, in Spring Lane, where the constitution of the YMCA of Boston was ratified on December 29, 1851.

Captain Thomas Valentine Sullivan, seaman and lay missionary, at age 30. He convened a meeting of 32 concerned Christian men from 20 congregations in Boston on December 15, 1851. He helped draft the constitution of the Boston association that was approved on December 29.

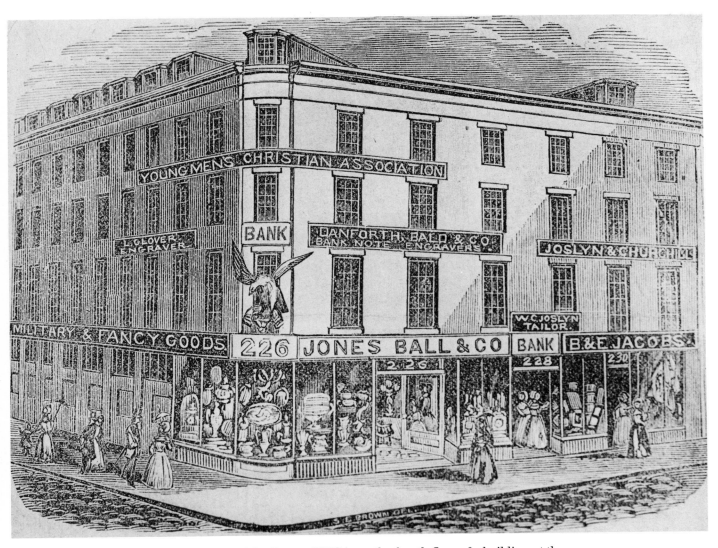

The first rooms of the Boston YMCA, on the fourth floor of a building at the corner of Summer and Washington streets. When the rooms were dedicated on March 11, 1852, members sang, to the tune of "Greenville":

Blest be this Association
　　In its object and its end,
Active still in the creation
　　of the Christian and the Friend!

Ever faithful to its mission,
　　Ever kind in its control,
Making still a clear impression
　　On the intellect and soul.

William Chauncy Langdon

"The great object of Christian Associations is the spiritual and mental growth of young men," Charles Demond of Boston told fellow delegates to the sixth annual convention of associations at Troy, New York, in 1859. "But," he added rhetorically, "if an old man or an old woman asks our prayers or our sympathy, shall we not pray or labor with such?"

For most of the 289 delegates to the convention, the answer was assumed: They worked especially for young men, but they were also "ready to enter upon any work which He shall open before us."

For William Chauncy Langdon, the "young father" of the new confederation of associations in the United States and Canada, the question was more troublesome and the answer given by the other delegates, painful.

From the District of Columbia association that he had helped found in 1852, Langdon struggled to persuade other associations to organize for mutual support. By correspondence and through personal visitation, he reasoned, cajoled, and badgered. By 1854, he eased the resistance of some larger associations which feared that the more numerous smaller associations would control any organization, no matter how carefully structured, and the confederation of associations was formed. He avoided the increasingly divisive question of slavery by creating "the unformulated understanding" that "sectional questions" would not be discussed. The understanding angered many, including the Toronto association, which eventually withdrew from the confederation over the issue. But it was this compromise that made the organization possible.

Religious revivals in 1858 and the simple human response to those in need led members of many associations to increase their "general work"—helping widows and orphans, teaching in mission schools. Some were preaching, and a few had even begun to criticize Protestant churches for their inability to cooperate in good

William Chauncy Langdon, who urged the creation of a voluntary confederation of Young Men's Christian Associations for "their mutual encouragement, co-operation, and more extended usefulness." That confederation is now the YMCA of the USA.

works. Langdon, who was being ordained in the Episcopal Church, feared that any conflict with the churches would destroy the confederation and tried to eliminate general work. At the 1858 convention at Charleston, he helped delegates resolve that "the true sphere" of association work was "the formation and development of Christian character and activity in young men."

That resolution stopped neither the general work nor debate about it. Langdon came to Troy to warn the delegates that "we are in danger of losing our original character." He introduced a resolution to limit association work to young men, and in the "warm debate" that followed, found himself alone in its defense. Finally, Cephas Brainerd, a young New York attorney attending his first convention, moved successfully to table the resolution. When a contrary motion passed without dissent, Langdon announced regretfully that he must withdraw from the convention. The presiding officer, George Stuart of Philadelphia, closed business at the session and asked Langdon to give the benediction. After he finished, it is said, many delegates, not a few in tears, crowded around him to wish him Godspeed.

Odeon Hall, at the corner of Main and Mohawk streets in Buffalo, New York, where the first meeting of the confederation was held in June 1854. Photo courtesy of the Buffalo and Erie County Historical Society.

Some of the 37 young men who were delegates to the first confederation meeting.

George Helme of New Orleans, who presided at the meeting.

William Rhees of the District of Columbia.

N. A. Halbert of Buffalo.

Samuel Lowry of Cincinnati.

William Neff of Cincinnati.

H. Thane Miller of Cincinnati.

The first association building erected
in the United States, at the corner of
Shroeder and Pierce streets in Baltimore. It was built in 1859 at a cost
of $7,000.

The famous and beloved "food wagon" patented by Jacob Dunton of Philadelphia and offered to the United States Christian Commission for its work during the Civil War. The coffee wagon, as it came to be known, was sent to the front at City Point, Virginia, where a whole division was under fire. It brought hot coffee to the soldiers there, "the first they had tasted in two weary days or more."

Chapter 2

This Sturdy Child of the YMCA

In November 1861, seven months after the Civil War began at Fort Sumter, representatives from 15 Young Men's Christian Associations met in New York City to decide how Northern associations could best "work together in aid of the soldiers." On November 15, they created the United States Christian Commission "to promote the spiritual and temporal welfare of the soldiers in the army and the sailors in the Navy, in cooperation with the chaplains." George Stuart, the founder and then president of the Philadelphia association, was named to chair the commission, which had 12 members.

During the next four years, the commission supervised 4,859 volunteers, called "delegates," who served an average of 37 days each. Forty-three of these delegates, including three women and five members of the commission itself, died during the war. The commission raised more than $6,000,000 and provided an equal amount in material and services. One innovative service was proposed by Mrs. Annie Wittenmyer of Iowa, who observed that sick and wounded soldiers needed special food, not the indigestible oily broths produced for them by soldier-cooks. The commission provided funds to establish "diet kitchen services," which she and her staff of 110 "experienced and competent" Christian women managed.

The commission placed special emphasis on religious work: During the war, delegates distributed 1,446,748 Bibles and 1,370,953 hymn books, preached 58,308 sermons, and held 77,744 prayer meetings. But the commission also realized, as George Stuart pointed out, that there is "a good deal of religion in a warm shirt and a good beefsteak." Its delegates delivered fresh bread and hot coffee to soldiers in battle and established a "strawberry fund" in New York to distribute fresh fruit to soldiers coming home. The commission printed and circulated detailed instructions for those who wanted to ship pickles, boiled cider, apple butter, and grated horseradish to camps. It reported faithfully dispensing these and other items, such as shirts, drawers, crackers, cordials, Jamaican ginger, condensed milk, and "Scriptures in German, French, and other foreign languages." Delegates also opened schools for colored soldiers, wrote letters for the wounded, and circulated books from loan libraries—excluding, of course, "all yellow-covered literature, lives of pirates and highwaymen, [and] works against Christ and country."

Separated from war by space and time, we might look upon such services as small, and some even comical. But to the soldiers in the field and to their families at home, these small gifts added to a "great humanitarian service," one that earned the nation's respect for the Young Men's Christian Association which created it.

Executive Mansion,

Washington, Dec. 12, 1861.

Rev. George H. Stuart
Chairman of Christian Commission
My dear Sir:

Your letter of the 11th Inst. and accompanying plan, both of which are returned as a convenient mode of connecting this with them, have just been received— Your Christian and benevolent undertaking for the benefit of the soldiers, is too obviously proper, and praise-worthy, to admit any difference of opinion— I sincerely hope your plan may be as successful in execution, as it is just and generous in conception.

Your Obt. Servt.
A. Lincoln.

A facsimile of a letter from President Abraham Lincoln to George Stuart, the chairman of the Christian Commission, approving the plan of the commission to serve soldiers.

George Stuart of Philadelphia, founder and president of the YMCA there at the time he became chairman of the Christian Commission.

The Christian Commission supply depot at Washington, D.C., where Bibles, hymnbooks, conserves [medicinal plants mixed with sugar], bandages, and the like were gathered for shipment to soldiers in the field.

The tent of the Christian Commission in the field.

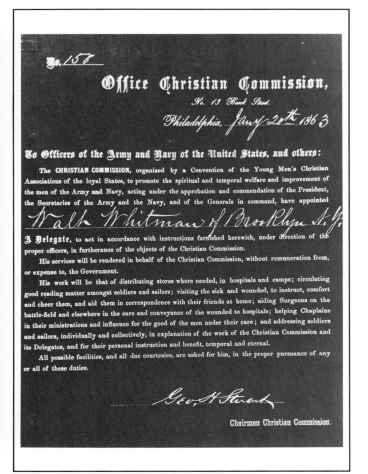

A document identifying Walt Whitman of Brooklyn, New York, as a delegate of the Christian Commission.

In *Specimen Days,* published in 1881, Whitman described his work for the Christian Commission:

During those years in hospital, camp, or field, I made over six hundred visits or tours, and went, as I estimate, counting all, among from eighty thousand to a hundred thousand of the wounded and sick, as sustainer of spirit and body in some degree, in time of need. These visits varied from an hour or two to all day or night; for with dear or critical cases I generally watched all night. Sometimes I took up my quarters in the hospital, and slept or watched there several nights in succession.

Those three years I consider the greatest privilege and satisfaction (with all their feverish excitements and physical deprivations and lamentable sights), and, of course, the most profound lesson of my life. I can say that in my ministerings I comprehended all, whoever came in my way, Northern or Southern, and slighted none. It aroused and brought out and decided undream'd of depths of emotion. It has given me my most fervent views of the true ensemble and extent of the States. While I was with wounded and sick in thousands of cases from New England States, and from New York, New Jersey, and Pennsylvania, and from Michigan, Wisconsin, Ohio, Indiana, Illinois, and all the Western States, I was with more or less from all the States, North and South, without exception.

I was with many from the border States, especially from Maryland and Virginia, and found, during those lurid years 1862-63, far more Union Southerners, especially Tennesseans, than is supposed. I was with many rebel officers and men among our wounded, and gave them always what I had, and tried to cheer them the same as any. I was among the army teamsters considerably, and indeed, always found myself drawn to them. Among the black soldiers, wounded or sick, and in the contraband camps, I also took my way whenever in their neighborhood, and did what I could for them.

[from "Walt Whitman as an Army Man." *Association Men,* April, 1920. p. 484.]

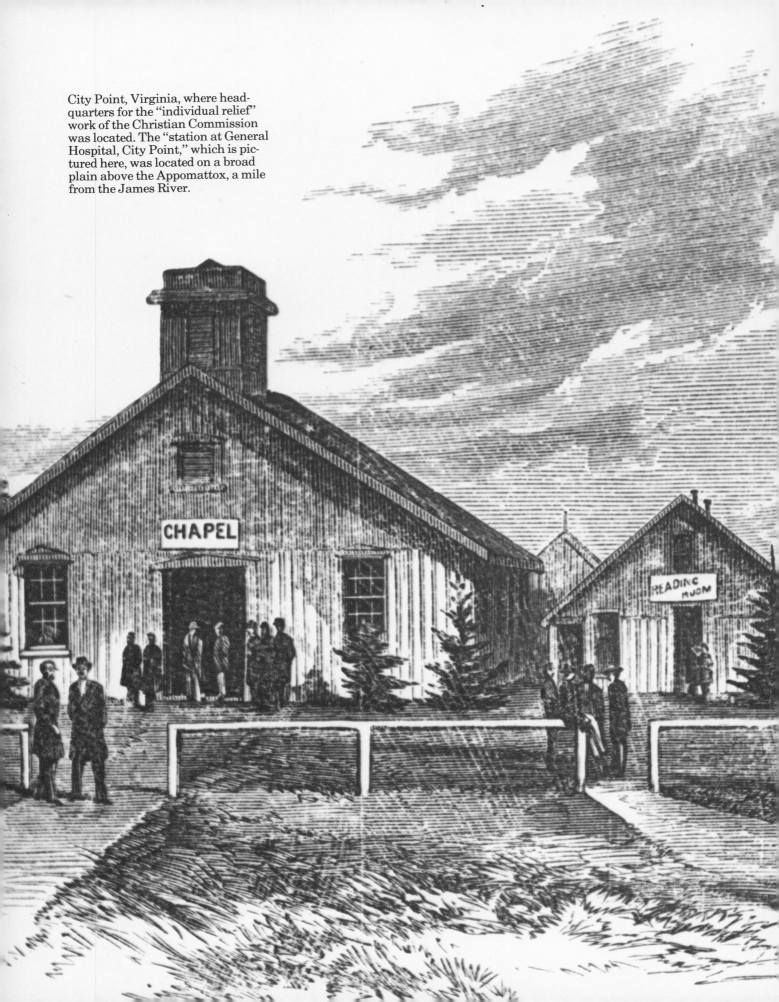

City Point, Virginia, where headquarters for the "individual relief" work of the Christian Commission was located. The "station at General Hospital, City Point," which is pictured here, was located on a broad plain above the Appomattox, a mile from the James River.

The Record of the Federal Dead

These pages are excerpts from a 200-page book published by the Christian Commission.

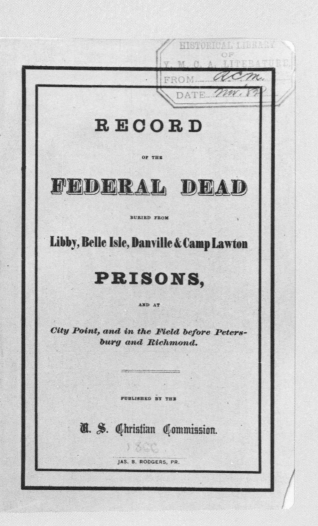

RECORD

OF THE

FEDERAL DEAD

BURIED FROM

Libby, Belle Isle, Danville & Camp Lawton

PRISONS,

AND AT

City Point, and in the Field before Petersburg and Richmond.

PUBLISHED BY THE

U. S. Christian Commission.

JAS. B. RODGERS, PR.

PREFACE.

The work of examining and cataloguing the graves of the heroes of the Secession War, in and around Richmond, was undertaken in behalf of friends at home, to save them the weary task of groping among the dead for their loved and lost ones. The results of the work, which was carried on by the Agents of the Christian Commission, under the direction of HEN. C. HOUGHTON, Chief of the Individual Relief Department, are embodied in the following pamphlet, which can lay claim to only an approximate accuracy. Further search might furnish additional particulars, and we doubt not that such search will be made. But even in aid of this, the record here given will be valuable.

DANVILLE.

On the 15th of May, 1864, two U. S. C. C. Agents—Messrs. Houghton and Williams—visited Danville, and obtained the following list, which dates from November 24, 1864, to April 28, 1865. The prisoners had been confined in four large factories. The cemetery is about a mile and a half from the town, and is well arranged. The graves are marked by head-boards, with the names legibly painted, and more care is evident than in any other Confederate prison burial-place. The bodies of any of our soldiers can be obtained—through Mr. Hill, of that city, undertaker—by their friends, at any time during the Fall.

The initial letters, after the date, indicate the disease of which each died. D. C.—Chronic Diarrhœa; F. T.—Typhoid Fever; V.—Small-pox; R. C.—Chronic Rheumatism; Pn.—Pneumonia; F. A.—Fever and Ague; E.—Erisypelas; B. C.—Chronic Bronchitis; H.—Liver Disease; H. C.—Chronic Liver Disease; D. A.—Acute Diarrhœa; C.—Consumption; V. F.—Varioloid; Pl.—Pleurisy; C.—Heart Disease; N.—Neuralgia; S.—Scurvy; F. C.—Congestive Fever; D.—Diphtheria; P.—Paralysis; Cat.—Catarrh.

Names of Federal sick and wounded who have died at Danville, Va., during the war:

E. Duan, B, 8th Mich., November, 24, 1863, D.
Fredelin Streetinwater, A, 19th U. S. I., November 26, 1863, D.
Nathaniel Fultz, K, 89th Ohio, November 27, 1863, D.
Elijah Terry, H, 42d Ill., November 27, 1863, F. T.
Aaron Cronk, K, 25th Mich., November 28, 1863, F. T.
A. Grinnels, K, 4th Ky. Cav., November 28, 1863, V.
A. P. Arnold, F, 4th Ky. Cav., November 28, 1864, V.
E. Case, C, 29th Ind., November 28, 1863, D. C.
J. A. Sidler, G, 87th Ind., November 29, 1863, V.
Joel Williams, H, 3d Ky., November 30, 1863, V.
Wm. Evans, I, 51st Ohio, November 30, 1863, D. C.
Corp. Wm. Brandt, I, 39th Ind., November 30, 1863, R. C.
Frank Gerstung, I, 112th Ill., December 1, 1863, F. T.
J. Askinburg, I, 16th U. S. I., December 2, 1863, D. C
James Connor, A, 79th Ohio, December 3, 1863, V.
Wm. Dinsmore, D, 51st Ill., December 4, 1863, V.

Frank Parker, F, 1st Tenn. Cav., December 4, 1863, V.
James Nally, H, 6th Ky. Cav., December 5, 1863, V.
John Johnson, C, 8th Mich., December 5, 1863, V.
Corp. W. A. Jones, C, 33d Ohio, December 5, 1863, D. C.
Sergt. Elihu Billings, I, 89th Ind., December 6, 1863, Pn.
Wm. Gambol, H, 18th U. S. I., December 6, 1863, Pn.
J. Newton, G, 73d Ohio, December 6, 1863, D. C
F. Leith, C, 68th Ind., December 6, 1863, D.C.
J. Cope, H, 21st Ill., December 6, 1863, F. A.
C. A. Brown, A, 19th Mass., December 7, 1863, Pn.
F. Brickford, D, 22d Mich., December 7, 1863, F. T.
W. Carroll, F, 8th Tenn. Cav., December 7, 1863, F. T.
R. Livingston, I, 82d Ind., December 7, 1863, V.
A. Allen, I, 14th Mich., December 8, 1863, D. C.
M. Brannon, K, 8th Mich., December 10, 1863, D. C.
J. Coyfort, C, 11th Tenn., December 10, 1863, D. C.
J. L. Beath, H, 89th Ohio, December 10, 1863, D. C.
H. Knapp, A, 22d Mich., December 10, 1863, Pn.
A. Howlett, F, 18th Ky., December 11, 1863, V.
W. W. Smith, I, 14th Mich., December 11, 1863, Pn.
G. T. Jennings, C, 11th Ky. Cav., December 11, 1863, F. T.
Thos. Nolan, A, 16th U. S. I., December 12, 1863, D. C.
H. T. Layfield, B, 59th Ohio, December 12, 1863, F. T.
W. R. Ford, I, 112 Ill., December 12, 1863, V.
John Sweaney, A, 8th Tenn. Cav., December 12, 1863, V.
John Ferguson, F, 8th Tenn. Cav., December 12, 1863, V.
M. Wilson, A, 1st Cav., December 13, 1863, D. C.
Jno. M. Evans, E, 35th Ohio, December 14, 1863 V.
O. Fall, D, 22d Mich., December 14, 1863, V.
J. Carson, G, 36th Ill., December 14, 1863, V.
J. Close, G, 25th Iowa, December 14, 1863, Pn.
J. Reder, B, 1st Ohio, December 15, 1863, D. C.
D. C. Chase, D, 8th Mich., December 15, 1863, D. C.
C. McDonald, A, 1st Wis., December 15, 1863, V.
M. Dougherty, C, 8th Kansas, December 15, 1863, F. T
T. H. Henry, G, 21st Ohio, December 15, 1863, Pn.
E. G. Browning, B, 3d Tenn. Cav., December 16, 1863, V.
C. Closson, C, 15th U. S. I., December 16, 1863, Pn.
W. Priest, A, 29th Ind., December 16, 1863, F. T.
J. Fryar, F, 8th Tenn. Cav., December 16, 1863, D. C.
H. H. Lee, B, 92d Ohio, December 16, 1863, V.
J. W. Gibbs, K, 92d Ohio, December 16, 1863, V.
H. Wheeler, D, 65th Ohio, December 16, 1863, V.
S. R. Howard, D, 65th Ohio, December 17, 1863, D. C.
J. Alison, D, 64th U. S., December 17, 1863, Pn.
S. Garner, C, 30th Ind., December 17, 1863, D. C.
R. B. Cunningham, B, 3d Tenn. Cav., December 17, 1863, V.
T. W. Shepard, I, 115th Ill., December 17, 1863, V.
John Lester, F, 90th Ohio, December 17, 1863, V.
J. Marshall, A, 28th Mass., December 18, 1863, Pn.
Morgan Presley, A, 8th Tenn. Cav., December 18, 1863, V.

2

Back of Meade Station, west.
A. J. Locke, F, ——

Between Picket Lines front of Fort Steadman.
I. C. Gray, ——

Near Meade Station.
J. T. Johnson.
Lewis Poole, K, 146th
E. Boothe, Purnell Cav.
Fred. Miller, D, 10th U. S Infantry.
Last three at Fort Steadman,

Half mile west of Parke Station.
George Rosisons, D, ——
Joshua T. Copper, ——
John Stenner, A, Purnell Legion.

Large yard west of Parke Station.
M. I. Moss.

Near the House of Mr. Kane.
H. Murphy.

Near Warren Station, on Weldon Rail-Road.
Alonzo Hetchum.

Near Patrick Station, to the south east.
Wm Huffman.
Lieut. H. G. Maclavish.

Yard near the last.
S. Hill.
David Fane——.

Yard near the R. R., at Patrick Station.
Fred Christ, Bat. F, 5th U. S. Art.

Yard east of last.
Corp. M. Flanders, G, 12th U. S. Infantry.
Corp. I. Barbur, H, 12th U. S. Infantry.
James Fow.
Jonas Kime, G, 11th U. S. Infantry.
Thos. Corcoran, A, 10th U. S. Infantry.
George Harris, A. 10th U. S. Infantry.

Near R. R. Bridge, Hatcher's Run.
T. O. Brien.

Near Spain House.
Milton Vauneler.

Near Sidney's House, near Five Forks.
—— O. Field, 5th Corps.

One mile East of Hancock's Station ; Timble's House.
Sergt C. H Howard, H, —— U. S. S. S.

Burksville Junction, Va.
Samuel T. Read, Orderlies Staff.
John M. Moore.

Buried, between Middletown and Strasburg, near Sperry's House.
Harvey Winters, B, 2d Conn. Art.

Buried between Kernstown and Newton, one and a half miles from Kernstown, near woods.
Patrick Delany, B, 2d Conn. Art.

Buried in Hospital burying-ground, near Patrick's Station.
Allen W. Barnet, A, 82d Pennsylvania.
Wm. Fransher, C, 82d Pennsylvania.
John Southmaid, E, 5th Wisconsin.
Wm. H. Averill, H, 37th Massachusetts.
Corp. Edward Vallette, D, 2d Rhode Island.
Joshua Gordon, E, 10th New Jersey.
S. Smith, E, 4th New Jersey.
Henry A. Strange, F, 2d Rhode Island.
Henry Cooker, A, 2d Pennsylvania Cav.
Alfred Tompkins, C, 1st New Jersey.
Quinton Bliss, B, 37th Massachusetts.
Jas. C. Carpenter, B, 95th N. Y.
David Kemper, I, 82d Pennsylvania.

Buried about three miles east of Burksville Junction, south of R. R. twenty rods from house used as 1st Div., Hd. Qrs., 6th A. C.
James Murray, C, 40th New Jersey.

Buried near Middletown.
John McGunnigle, K, 1st Maine.
Jas. W. Davis, K, 1st Maine.

Buried in Kernstown.
Carl. Busche, B, 43d N. Y.
Wm. A. Dow, F, 5th Vermont.
B. F. Whitney, K, 11th Vermont.
Jas. F. Toland, F, 102d Pennsylvania.

Buried in 2d Div. Hospital grounds, near Patrick's Station.
Jacob Hebrilge, G, 61st Pennsylvania.
Jos. Zihes, K, 4th Vermont.
Henry Cramer, K, 98th Pennsylvania.
Henry C. Libby, C, 1st Maine.
Jas. Cole, A, 77th N. Y.
Corp. Jos. Grow, E, 11th Vermont.
John Brazee, C, 93d Pennsylvania.
Henry C. Hadley, D, 11th Vermont.
Wm. S. Craft, A, 102d Pennsylvania.
Nathan W. Lemmon, A, 61st Pennsylvania.
—— Winegrove, —— 102d Pennsylvania.

Chapter 3

A Period of Beginnings

Only 59 associations, 2 of them in the South, survived the Civil War. They emerged, however, with remarkable energy and a national reputation for humanitarian service.

In the decade after the war, the associations, acting through their annual convention, defined their purpose as work "for young men, by young men." They voted, in effect, to limit active membership to those who were members of evangelical churches. The convention of 1866 created an executive committee, which replaced the central committee, and voted to place it in New York City, first experimentally, then permanently. The 1868 convention authorized the executive committee to hire its first secretary, Robert Weidensall, to promote association work along the Union Pacific Railroad lines. The next year, the executive committee hired Richard Morse, who edited *Association Monthly* until he became general secretary in 1872. By the end of the 1860s, there were more than 650 associations.

The most important change in those years was not one of numbers or of organizational structure but one of method of work. When the first associations began in London and the United States, members worked

Many of the 136 delegates to the ninth convention of the Young Men's Christian Associations of North America at Boston in 1864. These delegates, representing 28 associations, passed a resolution urging that a secretary or "some other officer" be appointed to "visit the several YMCA's in this land" to promote the movement.

through "earnest, personal effort" to reach the unconverted. Intense prayer and Bible study helped members and new converts grow together "in Grace and Bible knowledge" and to perform good works of Christian benevolence. Gradually and experimentally, associations began to offer young men other reasons to join their fellowship. They found that a gymnasium or a popular lecturer brought young men to them. As they reported their successes to each other at conferences and conventions, more associations added physical and social dimensions to the spiritual and intellectual work they were doing.

It wasn't until years later that Luther Halsey Gulick explained the significance of this development. In 1889 he first discussed his belief in the importance of the unity of spirit, mind, and body in the Christian personality. He proposed the inverted triangle as the emblem of the association and the symbol of that unity. In doing so, he articulated a philosophy of work that associations had been practicing since Robert Ross McBurney installed a gymnasium in New York.

Robert Weidensall, a former black-
smith and proud railroad worker, who
became the first field secretary of the
movement in 1868. The photos were
taken at Gettysburg, Pennsylvania,
when he was 24, and after he had
completed 50 years of association work
as the "best-loved man of the
brotherhood."

Richard Morse, a journalist and member of a distinguished New England family that included Samuel Morse, the inventor of the telegraph. The first photo was taken in 1873, just after he became the first national general secretary, the second after he had completed more than 50 years of association service.

Robert Ross McBurney, the "ideal secretary" of the New York association, led it and the movement to a fourfold program addressed to the spiritual, mental, physical, and social needs of young men.

Cephas Brainerd, an attorney and member of the New York association, who chaired the International Committee from 1867 to 1892. He was the "great chief justice of our American Associations."

The secretaries of the International Committee in 1883: *Back row, from left:* Luther Wishard, Claus Olandt, Thomas Cree. *Middle row:* Edwin Ingersoll, Erskine Uhl, Richard Morse, Robert Weidensall. *Front row:* Jacob Bowne, Henry Brown. This is the first national staff photo.

The first four secretaries of student
work, from left: Robert Weidensall,
Luther Wishard, Charles Ober, John R.
Mott.

"The birthplace of the Intercollegiate Movement of the American Young Men's Christian Associations," at Fourth and Chestnut streets in Louisville, Kentucky, 1877. Luther Wishard led a delegation of 25 students from 21 student associations (including three at black colleges) to Louisville, where the annual YMCA convention was being held. Delegates at the convention agreed to appoint a "corresponding secretary" to promote work among the colleges.

A group of secretaries and general secretaries for the state of Georgia, taken in Macon, August 22, 1895.

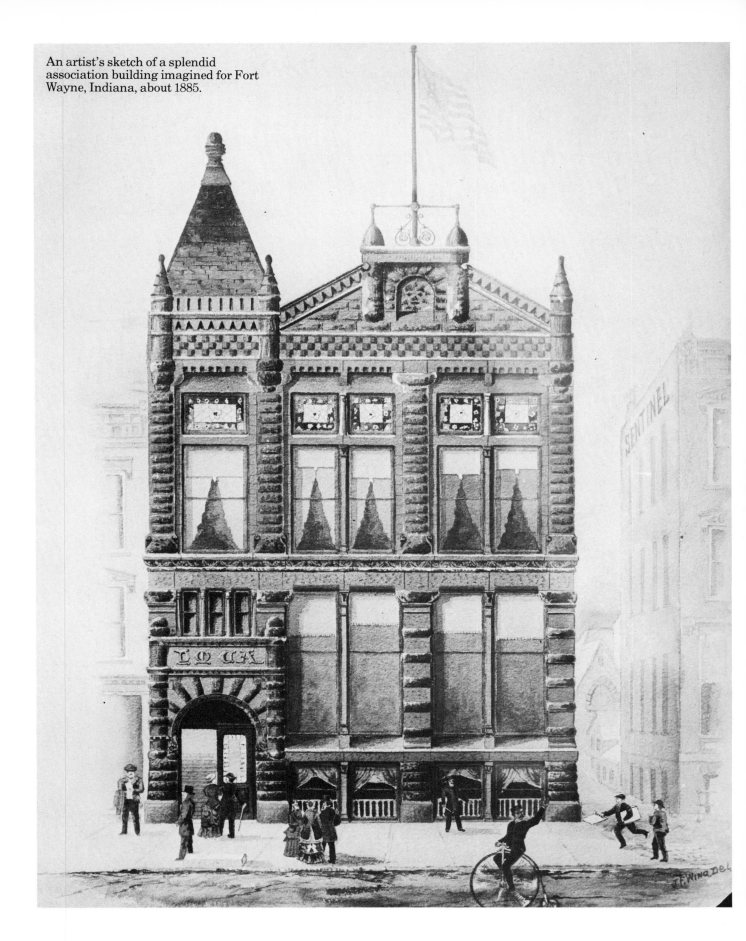

An artist's sketch of a splendid association building imagined for Fort Wayne, Indiana, about 1885.

Three "local centers of Christian affection" at Knoxville, Tennessee, top; Milwaukee, bottom; and Selma, Alabama, below, 1888. YMCA buildings, it was said, offered young men six days each week what they received at churches on the seventh only.

A carefully furnished dormitory room
at Sioux City, Iowa.

A Victorian parlor in Milwaukee,
probably in the 1880s.

The hall and lounging room of the
Harrisburg, Pennsylvania, association, probably in the 1880s.

The Harrisburg association building.

The reading room of the Harrisburg association.

An afternoon institute at the
Bloomington (Illinois) association,
May 22, 1905.

Gym in Milwaukee in pre-basketball
days. Note the chandelier.

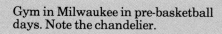

Members of an unidentified local association in the late nineteenth century. The gentlemen in above photo subscribe to the idea that "morals are muscularly made."

Notwithstanding the widespread fear of "popular amusements," some shot pool at the West Side Branch of the Chicago association.

Others worked more diligently, as did those in this shop at Portland, Oregon, 1902.

James Naismith (in street clothes)
with members of what is believed to be
the first "basket ball" team in the
United States, at Springfield College, 1891.

Sumner Dudley, the father of camp-
ing, with friends at camp in Westport,
New York, 1887. Dudley is seated in
the front, holding the mallet.

The School for Christian Workers at
Springfield, Massachusetts, for the
training of secretaries of the YMCA,
about 1885.

Jacob Titus Bowne

Jacob Bowne was a collector. His hobby was collecting stone implements used by native Americans, and when he gave his collection of "Indian antiquities" to the Science Museum of Springfield, Massachusetts, just before his death in 1925, it was one of the best in the country.

Bowne's life work was collecting the historical records of the lay Christian impulse embodied in the YMCA. He began modestly, in 1877, to gather early reports to use in his association work in Newburgh, New York. Over the next 30 years, he acquired and saved thousands of manuscripts, newsletters of local and foreign associations, and publications of other organizations also engaged in lay Christian work for young men. His treasures included sermons on vice preached in colonial New England and reports of British societies for wayfaring seamen. These antiquities he left in trust to the International Committee for the benefit of all the associations of North America.

Jacob Bowne was also a teacher. He is known as the "father of professional education" in the YMCA, which began modestly as the Ten Day Fellowship Meeting he offered at Newburgh for young men preparing to become YMCA secretaries. In 1883 the International Committee hired him to head its secretarial bureau, and in 1885 he moved to Springfield to direct training of apprentice secretaries in the YMCA department of the new School for Christian Workers. That department became Springfield College, where Bowne spent 38 years as a faculty member and college librarian.

Bowne's students and colleagues at Springfield knew him as a gentle

Jacob Bowne, the father of professional education in the YMCA and the first archivist of the movement, 1879.

Quaker with a "sincere mind and loving heart." They remembered that in matters of theology and association method, he remained adaptable. He treasured the artifacts of the past, but he refused to let his mind be "entirely hedged in" by the past. His friends and students also remembered his characteristic modesty. Whenever one of them tried to thank "Jake" for a kindness, he turned the gratitude aside. "Pass it along," he would say of his kindness and his collections as well.

Chapter

Making Christ Known to All Men

For 26 days in July 1886, nearly 250 students from 96 colleges attended the first national YMCA student summer conference. Luther Wishard, student secretary for the International Committee, organized the conference and persuaded evangelist Dwight Moody to lead it. The conference was held on the grounds of a boys school at Mount Hermon, near Northfield, Massachusetts, where Moody lived.

John R. Mott, then an undergraduate at Cornell University, attended. Twenty-five years later, even as the busy, burdened general secretary of the Interna-

tional Committee, he could recall vividly what the conference inspired.

The organizers had deliberately created an unhurried atmosphere, he remembered. In the morning, students gathered in small groups to discuss methods of association work among students. At a daily "platform" meeting, Moody led their study of the Gospel of Saint Matthew and invited one or two of his friends to preach. In the afternoon, students prayed or meditated, or walked in the woods above the Connecticut River. There was ample time to listen for God's

Delegates to the Mount Hermon conference, 1886. John R. Mott is in the back row, just left of center in dark spot. Seated in chairs in the front row are Dwight Moody, Edwin Ingersoll, Luther Wishard, and an unidentified colleague. "And He said to them, 'Go into all the world and preach the Gospel to all creation.'"

voice and to build their faith in Him.

Almost two weeks after the conference opened, a few students began to meet separately to pray for the foreign missions. Some began to find it "impossible to pray without work" and signed the missionary pledge: "We are willing and desirous, God permitting, to become foreign missionaries." By the last day of the conference, 99 students had signed the pledge.

The morning after the conference adjourned, the 99 crowded together in a small room. "While we were kneeling in that closing period of heart-burning prayer," Mott said, "the hundredth man came in and knelt with us."

That "wonderful student missionary uprising" at Mount Hermon, Mott said, inspired a generation of students to work for the evangelization of the entire world. Out of their intensity, he believed, grew the Student Volunteer Movement for Foreign Missions and the World's Student Christian Federation. From it came the foreign work of the YMCA.

The delegation from Cornell University to the Mount Hermon conference in a photograph taken after they returned to Ithaca, New York. John R. Mott is in the middle row at the left.

Barnes Hall at Cornell University, home of the student Christian union and the student YMCA.

David McConaughy graduated from Gettysburg College and served as general secretary of the Harrisburg and Philadelphia associations. He sailed for Madras in 1889 and spent the next 13 years as a foreign secretary there.

D. Willard Lyon, the son of Presbyterian missionaries, was born in China and educated at Wooster College in Ohio. From 1895 to 1930 he served as foreign secretary in China.

Myron A. Clark, a graduate of
Macalester College in St. Paul,
Minnesota, was the first foreign
secretary to serve in South America,
in 1891. He is pictured with Francisca
Pereira de Moraes, the Brazilian
woman he married, and their
three children.

Max Yergan, a secretary of the
colored men's department of the International Committee, served in India,
France, and in East Africa during
World War I. In 1920 he went to South
Africa as the first black secretary
there. He left association work in 1936,
largely to protest the racial policies of
the South African government.

Those leaving for foreign work were known as "outgoing secretaries." This group was going out to India in 1911.

Mrs. Brockman and son Allen Clark.

Fletcher Sims Brockman, who took his
wife and baby son to China in 1898.

Be Not Afraid

Fletcher Sims Brockman, who was born in Virginia in 1867, graduated Phi Beta Kappa from Vanderbilt University in 1891. For the next six years he worked for the International Committee, traveling as a student secretary in Southern states. In 1898, at age 31, he went to Nanking, China, as a foreign secretary.

Brockman became general secretary of the National Committee of the China Young Men's Christian Associations in 1901. He held that position until 1915, when he returned to the United States to serve as associate general secretary of the International Committee. Shortly after he returned, he gave a speech on the outreach of the YMCA in which he described his small part in the evangelization of the world. This is an excerpt from the speech:

It is a little over 17 years ago now, a cold winter night, midnight, and I was dropped with my wife and baby on a muddy flat in the interior of China. I shall never forget the darkness of the night nor my feelings. I had expected to go up to Nanking...to carry the Young Men's Christian Associations to a people that I knew not and did not understand....My friends had said good-bye to me, and a bunch of three of us, Robert Lewis and Robert Gailey and I, had started almost jauntily over to this country and over the Pacific, to organize the Young Men's Christian Association among four hundred millions of people, joining over there one other Secretary, Mr. Lyon, who had preceded us. It seemed very easy to make the Chinese understand the outreach of the Young Men's Christian Association and it seemed very good to be a part of the outreach of the Young Men's Christian Association, but this night on a muddy flat, up in the interior of China, attempting to go into a city where I was to be alone and so far from every other secretary that I could not expect to see them within six months, and the great iron gates at Nanking closed so that after 7 o'clock at night it was not possible for you to get into the City at all, and I had to sit with my wife and baby in a little hovel over a coal brazier, shivering in the night, to carry the outreach of the Young Men's Christian Association. It was the beginning, gentlemen, of a disillusion.

...[But] I have not told the worst yet; I have not told that night when I was fleeing from the Interior with my wife and two little children then, whom God had given us, and how we rushed down to our old home at Nanking and found the Viceroy there, having disobeyed the Empress Dowager and making strenuous efforts to save our lives and not to carry out the edict of the Empress Dowager, to cut our heads off, and he had the troops surround our home to guard us....I looked at my wife, and said, I have done it, I have brought her into the Dragon's Den, and those two little innocent sleeping babes whom God had entrusted to my care as their father, and I brought them to what would probably be worse than death.

And gentlemen, there swept over my soul, if I must confess it, a doubt so deep and agonizing that I cannot think of anything else to equal it, unless my soul shall be lost at last. It seemed to me that I could see Hell itself that morning.

The Outreach, The Outreach of the Association; it seemed to me to be a mockery. I remember I said to myself, "Why have I done it. Why couldn't I have stayed at home. I will be killed, but that doesn't matter. Who cares anything about his own life, but to have brought these three innocent persons who have entrusted their lives to me, to put them into this. Haven't I been a fiend instead of a representative of what was best to do?"...It was an agonizing moment, but it was gone, and there swept through my soul something to which every atom of my being responded with the rhythm of its entire nature, something that was deeper than my very heart itself, if possible, something that was closer and more real than my own hand, something that said to me: "I have sent thee, be not afraid."

A sketch of the "Empire State," built by the New Jersey Works in 1834.

Railroad workers with the New York and New England Line, number 4, of New Haven, Connecticut.

The New York Central and Hudson Line, number 871, a Class C-a engine built at the Schenectady Works in 1890.

Chapter 5

In the Path of the Steam Horse

The railroad was a "source of wonder" to nine-teenth-century Americans. Almost from the day the first engine chugged on a short journey, in August of 1829, they knew its possibilities for speed and power. When the golden spike was driven into a railroad tie at Promontory Point in Utah in 1869, it seemed to join the country as it connected the east and west lines. Small networks of rail lines grew up quickly, and in their "ceaseless shuttling," cities and towns came closer. The rugged men who built the lines and drove the trains were adventurers and heroes.

The railroad was a magical, if earthbound, carpet for the new Christian associations as well. Their first employed agent, Robert Weidensall, was a proud rail-road man who liked to tell that he helped build the first car that crossed the Rockies. His early work followed the lines of the Union Pacific. Local arrangements for the numerous conventions and conferences of the associations always began with a discussion of train schedules and rate privileges.

Association members used railroads for 20 years before Henry Stager formed the first railroad associa-tion, in Cleveland in 1872. Stager, a train dispatcher there, decided to do so one day as he watched a body being carried from the Cleveland station. "Who's that?" he heard a bystander ask. Oh, it's "only a railroad man," was the response.

Railroad associations were almost magically suc-cessful. They sponsored Bible classes and lectures and the usual programs of city associations. They also offered first aid classes and clean beds, good food, and hot or cold baths at any time of the day or night. The reaction of employees prompted employers to support the work generously. Cornelius Vanderbilt gave funds and also led Sunday services at Grand Central Terminal. President Theodore Roosevelt showed up at Topeka to lay the cornerstone and then stayed, it is said, to shake the hands of 1,400 members of the railroad brotherhoods.

If the railroad associations' success was built on the cooperation of employers and workers, its greatest difficulties came when that cooperation broke down, as it did increasingly in the late nineteenth century. In labor conflicts, one leader said, the association was caught "between the upper and the nether millstone" of the economic order. During strikes, employers wanted the associations to provide facilities and services to those hired to replace striking workers. Workers on strike wanted the associations to deny services to strikebreakers. The associations were caught between those they served and those whose support made the services possible.

In response, uneasily, association leaders decided that the best course was "straight down the middle of the road." The railroad associations would provide services to all employees, no matter when they were hired or if they were striking. Then, because the compromise unsettled them, they also resolved to work harder to build "right relations" between employers and workers.

THE CLEVELAND, OHIO, RAILROAD STATION, 1872
BIRTHPLACE OF THE RAILROAD "Y"

John Pixley Munn, personal physician to the Astors, Goulds, and Vanderbilts, was chairman of the committee for railroad work. As such, he traveled the rail systems extensively on "expeditionary campaigns" to promote association work.

Jay Gould, member of the prominent New York family and a patient of Dr. Munn, frequently rode the rails with the good doctor.

A reading room in a railroad association, probably in New York City.

The First Aid Club of the West Albany Railroad association, 1904. A similar association in Columbus, Ohio, opened its work with "an iron woven cot with air mattress, a canvas stretcher constructed with handles so that it could be carried into a coach door, a small hand chest supplied with lint, bandages and old muslin, and bottles containing camphor, ether and other remedies."

Woe Unto Those Who Are at Ease in Zion

State and national secretaries, who were responsible for supervising local associations, lived complicated lives. In the good times, they helped an association plan a new building or brought news of a new piece of athletic equipment. Occasionally a secretary enjoyed the luxury of leading a Bible class or praying privately with a young man. When a secretary had to bring news of scarce funds or an admonition from a state committee that had caught the scent of theological deviation, life was harder.

Railroad secretaries shared this familiar mix of tasks. In his splendid history, *The Story of the Railroad "Y"*, John Moore recalled one incident particularly "fraught with peril to the future of the Movement." With his tongue firmly in his cheek, he described what might have been the last encounter with a particular form of vice.

Moore, then a secretary employed by the New York state association, was at a dinner meeting of the state committee at the home of its chairman, Lucien Warner. There the group learned that the railroad association at Mechanicville had, to the scandal of some in the community, installed a billiard table. It was near the turn of the century, he said, and Protestant moralists had softened considerably on the dangers of popular "amusements," but the prejudice against billiards lingered.

As consternation at the table increased, Moore, no doubt the junior secretary present, was dispatched—from the middle of the dinner—to bring the deviating association to heel. He spent the night at the New York station and on the train, and he reached Mechanicville the next morning, tired and hungry. Moore negotiated through the day with the local secretary and his board, who apparently could not see a threat to the moral order in a billiard table. After reasoning with them, Moore tried a mix of "entreaty, cajolery, and warning." He didn't explain which approach worked, but finally, he reported, the offending table was locked in a closet.

"I returned to New York," he wrote, "aglow with the pleasurable feeling one has who believes he has rendered a great and enduring service for a cause."

Thomas Wakeman was imprisoned in 1862 after a battle in the war named for his father—Chief Little Crow. He was originally sentenced to be hanged, but because of his age—he was 16—his sentence was commuted. In jail he converted to Christianity and when he was released, returned to his people to found Christian associations.

John Eastman, another founder of Christian associations among the Sioux Indians in South Dakota.

Chapter 6

Men of Color

In the mid-nineteenth century, race was "the vexed problem" for the Young Men's Christian Association, as it was the rest of the country. It vexed, one suspects, because the leaders who made the compromises they knew were necessary, knew their Scriptures as well.

In the meantime, before the home missionaries arrived, people of color set out to help themselves. Anthony Bowen, who worked in the government patent office with William Chauncy Langdon, established an association for colored men in the District of Columbia in 1853. In both the North and the South, leaders of black communities, especially in the churches, led and supported association efforts for their young men. On the plains, Sioux Indians read the Gospel of John and determined for themselves "the rules of Jesus." The International Committee, which prided itself in numbering all the associations in the country, was surprised to find the existence of these associations.

Historical records of work with people of color reflect a slow advance from colored men's work to inter-racial services and deeper respect for other cultures. The documents of that progress are full of petition and response, cautious advice and careful statement of "difficulties." The photographs tell a different story, one full of strength, dignity, and the capacity for self-help.

Charles Eastman, a physician, was the International Committee's first Indian secretary, from 1895 to 1898.

Arthur Walking Horse Tibbetts, a graduate of Springfield College, who led association work among the Sioux Indians from 1898 to 1907.

Stephen Jones, International Committee Indian secretary after 1907.

The association at White Clay, Pine Ridge Reservation, South Dakota.

An association meeting of an unidentified group of native Americans.

Three generations of the Bull family, relatives of Chief Sitting Bull and members of the association.

Participants at the first Indian
students conference at Estes Park,
Colorado, June 1914.

Participants in the annual Indian students conference at Estes Park, June 1919.

The first division of the boys club at Virginia Union University in Richmond.

The cabinet of the association at Stillman Institute in Tuscaloosa, Alabama, 1922-1923.

E. V. C. Eato of New York City, first black delegate to an annual convention, 1867. He was given a standing ovation.

A volunteer Bible study group at Alcorn, Mississippi, 1918.

The association building at Newport News, Virginia, "where the men and boys spend the evening."

An association of railroad workers at
Bluefield, West Virginia.

The North Carolina, Virginia, and District of Columbia delegations to the 1913 student conference at King's Mountain, North Carolina. At King's Mountain, said Addie Hunton, "Many of these youths caught their first clear vision of the Kingdom of God here on earth and started out with a valiant and glorious faith to find their places in it."

William Alphaeus Hunton, first black secretary of the colored men's department of the International Committee.

William Alphaeus Hunton

At the annual YMCA convention in 1876, which celebrated 25 years of association work in North America, a delegate introduced a resolution to "put a man in the field" to promote association work among colored men. Stuart Robinson of Louisville, Kentucky, seconded the motion and offered $50 for field expenses. Sir George Williams, the convention's honored guest, offered $100.

That same year, the executive committee employed a white man, General George Johnston, to travel in the South to learn if white leaders would support such work. They did, and in 1879, the committee hired Henry Brown, a white minister, to work in the field. For 10 years, Brown "met with encouraging success," but as one leader observed, the sacred association principle of developing work in a field by using men of that field had not been followed. The work, he said, was "waiting for the right man." That man was William Alphaeus Hunton.

The son of a slave who had purchased his own freedom, Hunton was born and educated in Canada. He became an active member of the Ottawa Young Men's Christian Association and held a "secure

position" with the Bureau of Indian Affairs there. Members of the International Committee who learned of his character and Christian commitment arranged that he be offered the position of general secretary of the colored association at Norfolk, Virginia, in 1888. Before he accepted the offer, the committee's general secretary, Richard Morse, warned him of the significant "social sacrifices" he would make by leaving the more tolerant society of Canada for the United States. Hunton knew the call to Norfolk was God's will, he said, and he accepted it without question.

Hunton had served at Norfolk only three years when the International Committee asked him to join its staff. In 1891 he began 25 years' work. He built the colored men's department and its staff. He established or assisted 100 associations in black colleges. He was friend and adviser to young black leaders, among them Max Yergan, Jesse Moorland, and Channing Tobias. Underlying his association work was his belief that if people could "see clearly," they would "live honestly." He worked to help the races "see" each other, so they could transcend the "traditions of

prejudice and hate."

In his 25 years, Hunton faced what he and his biographer and wife, Addie Hunton, called "difficulties" and "discouragements," polite terms for prejudice and hostility and the equally painful indifference of the majority. He dealt with them, Addie Hunton said, by the "habit of serenity" and his faith that "reality, however crude and even cruel, could by patient effort be somehow lifted to the realm of idealism."

He wanted others to share his faith and his life work. In his last public address, which he made to delegates to the World's Student Christian Federation meeting at Lake Mohonk in New York in 1913, he concluded with this hope:

Pray with us that there shall come to the heart of the world not only an intelligent interpretation of the brotherhood of man, but a spiritual acceptance of it, so that speedily there may dawn a glorious morning when man shall not judge his fellowman by color, race, tradition or any of the accidents of life but by righteousness and truth and unselfish service to humanity.

Soldiers playing ball in France.

Chapter 7

Wherever the Soldier Goes, the Secretary Follows

On April 6, 1917, the United States declared war on Germany. That same day, John R. Mott, the general secretary of the International Committee, who was never faint-hearted when there was Christian work to be done, took the YMCA into war. Without consulting his associates, Mott wired President Woodrow Wilson to volunteer "the full service of the Association Movement."

The government asked the YMCA to take responsibility for canteen operations. Associations had been helping prisoners of war from belligerent nations since 1914—and continued to do so through and after the war—but this commitment was dramatically greater. To meet its obligation, the YMCA raised more than $150,000,000. It mobilized nearly 26,000 secretaries, 10 percent of them women, to serve abroad under the red triangle. The secretaries worked in Siberia, Poland, Germany, and other countries touched by war. Four of them died in action, and three died of wounds suffered in battle. Three hundred received citations for bravery.

To supply the canteens of France, the YMCA imported staples such as flour and sugar. It established "factories" to make what soldiers needed and wanted. There were 3 candy factories; 8 jam factories, which manufactured 2,000,000 tins; and 20 biscuit factories, which churned out 10,160,000 packages. The YMCA originally imported baseball bats from the United States for soldiers to use on their foreign diamonds. When bats could no longer be shipped, and with the "endless inventiveness" of the associations, secretaries opened their own baseball bat factory. It wasn't Louisville hickory, one secretary reported, but the bats worked.

Secretaries carried cigarettes to the front. They showed movies in leave areas and wrote letters for soldiers who were wounded or too sick to write for themselves. The thousands of small kindnesses and comforts they offered added to a great humanitarian service, one which earned for the secretaries under the red triangle the same national respect earned by the delegates of the Christian Commission 50 years before.

"Doughnuts for doughboys" are made by the staff of this YMCA factory in France.

"When all beds were filled, sailors or soldiers could sleep where they willed in the Y." These sailors are sleeping in a YMCA transportation hut.

In a "foyer," a French Young Men's Christian Association, during World War I.

This secretary dons a gas mask during an alert and continues his work from behind the canteen counter.

The exterior of a YMCA canteen dug-out situated 150 yards from enemy lines.

A YMCA dog who carried cigarettes to men on the firing line.

Alfred Stokes, YMCA secretary, distributing smokes to a wiring party at the front in France. Stokes was cited for bravery in aiding wounded men under heavy fire.

A few of the 2,600 women secretaries who served in France, at a station behind the lines.

General John Pershing, commander-in-chief of the American Expeditionary Forces, with YMCA workers attached to the Ninth Army Corps in France, 1919.

The YMCA woman distributing cigarettes to soldiers at Chateau-Thierry is identified on the photographs as Rebecca Ely. However, only Gertrude Ely is listed among the 26,000 names of YMCA staff in France in World War I; she was awarded the Croix de Guerre by the French government.

Grace Cleveland Porter, who indeed was "Amazing Grace." She served as "directress of service of recreation" under the auspices of the YMCA in Rome, overseeing work in 20 hospitals for the Italian Army.

Marguerite Standish Cockett, a physician, could not serve in the United States Army. In 1916, instead, she purchased an automobile and had it shipped to Italy where she drove it in the ambulance service. The next year, the YMCA invited her to work in canteens in France.

A group of women canteen workers in France. Marguerite Cockett is in the front row, left. Next to her is Hope Butler.

Addie Hunton with her soldiers in France, standing in "God's falling light."

Re-burying the Dead

Addie Hunton, the widow of William Hunton, went to France in 1918 as a YMCA secretary. There she walked beside colored soldiers who fought in a segregated army in a war to make the world safe for democracy. She witnessed heroism and racism and the loneliness, pain, and hungers of young men.

When she returned to the United States after the war, she and her friend Kathryn Johnson recorded their experiences. No episode in their book is more moving than their description of the final assignment given the colored battalions: the "gruesome, repulsive and unhealthful task" of re-burying the soldiers who had lain scattered on French battlefields during the winter of 1918.

We looked upon these soldiers of ours—the splendid 813th, 815th and 816th Pioneer Regiments and the numerous fine labor battalions—as they constructed the cemeteries at Romagne, Beaumont, Thiencourt, Belleau Woods, Fere-en-Tardenois and Soissons. We watched them as they toiled day and night, week after week, through drenching rain and parching heat. And yet these physical ills were as naught compared with the trials of discrimination and injustices that seared their souls like hot iron, inflicted as they were at a time when these soldiers were rendering the American army and nation a sacred service. Always in those days there was a fear of mutiny or rumors of mutiny. We felt most of the time that we were living close to the edge of a smoldering crater....

Rations were often scarce and poor at Romagne because we were so far from supplies, hence we prepared and served food for the soldiers all day long. But this was but a small task compared with that of keeping the men in good spirits and reminding them again and again of the glory of the work they had in hand. Always, whether in the little corner set aside in the Y barracks as our reception room, or among the books they liked so well to read, whether by the side of the piano or over the canteen, we were trying to love them as a mother or a dear one would into a fuller knowledge and appreciation of themselves, their task and the value of forbearance.

[from Addie W. Hunton and Kathryn M. Johnson. *Two Colored Women with the American Expeditionary Forces*. Brooklyn, Brooklyn Eagle Press, 1920. Copyrighted by Hunton and Johnson. pp.235-236.]

The YMCA float in the Boys Day Parade at Omaha, Nebraska, May 1, 1924. The float won first place for its slogan.

Chapter 8

Building Boys Is Better Than Mending Men

Once the associations began in the 1860s to define their work as "for young men, by young men," they inevitably extended that work to the boys from whom the young men grew. By 1869 the Salem (Massachusetts) association created a separate boys work department. In 1881 Buffalo hired Ellen Brown to teach boys in night school. She became the first boys work secretary, a position she held until 1901.

Early boys work was directed primarily at "employed boys." Association efforts centered on factories and other places where boys were employed. As individual states gradually increased the age of compulsory school attendance, there were fewer such boys. Work began to focus more on the schools. Hi-Y was born.

At the same time, associations began to shift their emphasis from the disadvantaged boy laborer to the boy in the broad middle class. Let us keep the normal from the whirlpool, one secretary urged.

The program most symbolic of that interest was the father-and-son movement that the YMCA created. In 1909 B. M. Russell, a boys work secretary in Providence, Rhode Island, arranged a father-and-son banquet for 300 participants. It was a stunning success. By 1913 the Cleveland association had persuaded the mayor to proclaim December 26 as Father-and-Son Day. He urged mayors of other cities to do the same. Three years later, the Cleveland association promoted banquets in 200 churches in the city. By 1924 more than 3,000,000 had participated in the banquets. It was, one historian observed, a "spectacular meteor racing through the churches" and the associations.

The idealized boy who was in danger of being lost, and Nick Mellick, a Syrian newsboy, who won the Bible-telling contest sponsored by the association in Pittsburgh.

A factory class for boys on "Christian Teachings on Social Questions."

A boys group at a cotton mill.

The Y-Industry club of Buffalo, New York, which met at the factory where the boys worked.

Detroit "Y" Boys - One Division.

"If you are going to do anything for the average man, you have to begin before he is a man."

Theodore Roosevelt.

The YMCA newsboys club in Youngstown, Ohio. Note the motto at the left rear: "Only ignorant boys swear."

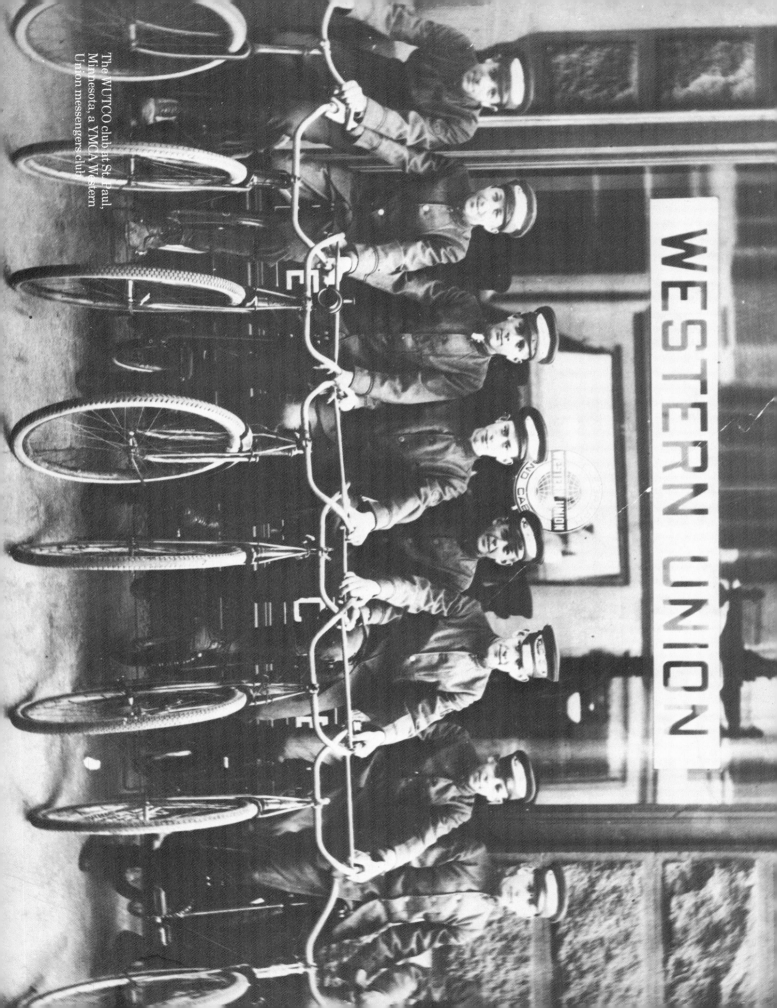

The WUTCO club at St. Paul, Minnesota, a YMCA Western Union messengers club

The Laverne Post Lights, an employed boys basketball team at a Chicago YMCA, 1926.

LAVERNE POST LIGHTS
CHICAGO CENTRAL C.E.B. 1926

One of the first employed boys junior brotherhoods, at Lawrence, Massachusetts, December 1917.

A conference of employed older boys (age 15-17) where major Christian themes were presented and discussed.

An unidentified Bible study class taking the national examinations, April 10, 1926. This class of 62 boys held 25 meetings to prepare for the exam.

"The boys have no place to go after school to spend their leisure moments. Our small room is crowded every evening with these bright and promising boys. There are about a thousand such boys in San Francisco Chinatown."

The annual father-and-son banquet at South Bend, Indiana.

At a father-and-son banquet in Denver, 1925.

The Central Hi-Y at Grand Rapids, Michigan, 1917-1918.

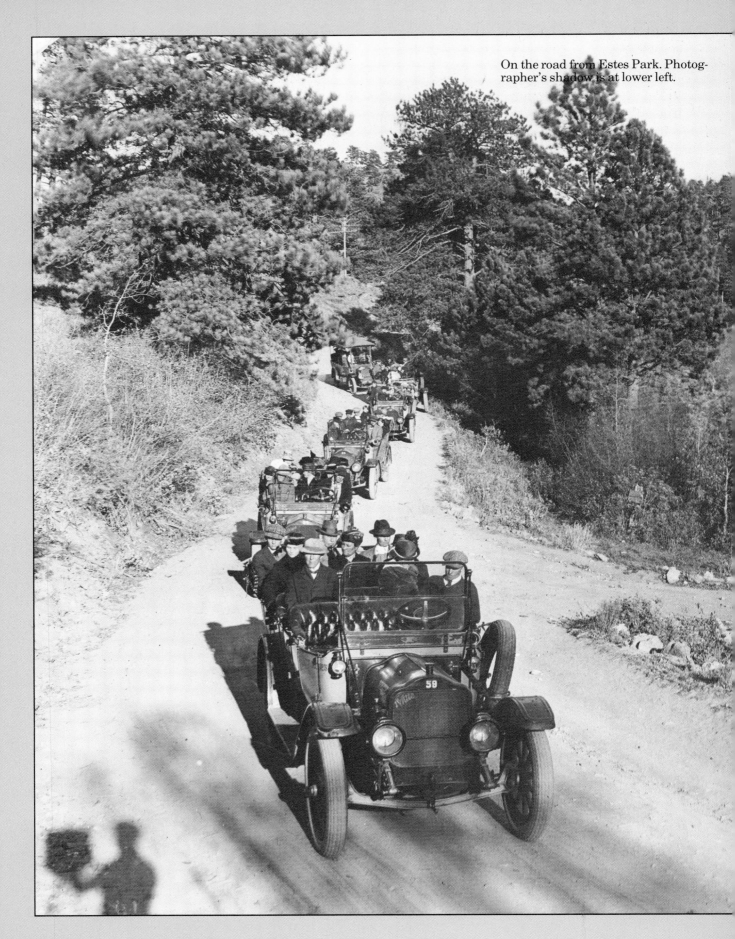

On the road from Estes Park. Photographer's shadow is at lower left.

This Epochal Meeting

Members of the YMCA community have traditionally enjoyed conferences—and conventions, summer schools, institutes, and assemblies as well. Such gatherings did more than satisfy the urges of gregarious spirits, however. They provided members of a national community with a chance to share "knowledge, inspired power, high purpose, and true fellowship" that flowed and overflowed among them.

Few meetings overflowed more than the third Assembly of YMCA Workers with Boys held at Estes Park, Colorado, in June 1925. Four hundred delegates met for eight days. Their theme was "new frontiers."

Delegates shared a conviction that an old order was passing. "We have come to feel," said one boys worker, "that Personal evangelism is not a thing of a moment, a single commitment or decision, but is a life process...a process of 'being and doing'—a development rather than the decision of a moment." In the new order, Christianity was not a gift the worker brought to boys but a goal that they, with his help, sought. Work *with* boys, not *for* them, was the watchword.

This shift in approach required new methods of work, and conference leaders, full of "vision and daring," showed delegates a few. The conference was deliberately less structured. There were fewer formal presentations and more discussion, especially in small groups. Leaders guided and helped rather than directed discussion. It was, an observer commented, an exercise in democratic methods of group work.

It was also heady stuff. Delegates left Estes Park exhilarated, full of a hope that few had had since so much hope died in the Great War. Delegates had reaffirmed their Christian purpose: to help boys grow in grace and work in God's name. Now, they believed, they knew how they could make—or help—it happen.

The association at St. Petersburg, Russia, which was called the Society for Co-operating with St. Petersburg Young Men in the Attainment of Moral and Physical Development.

Chapter 9

Serving in the World

The foreign work of the YMCA began in "the student missionary uprising" at Mount Hermon. When the first YMCA foreign secretaries sailed for India and Japan in 1889, they were part of a crusade for "the evangelization of the world in a generation." Theirs came to be a voyage of both service and discovery.

Foreign secretaries participated in the great crusade by establishing associations in other lands. They served only in countries to which they had been invited, and their first effort in a new place was to find and cultivate local leaders. The American movement supported its secretaries in the field and helped raise funds for buildings there, but local associations overseas were self-supporting.

If American movement policy required a uniform, general approach, local needs and opportunities led to programs remarkable for their inventiveness and diversity. Local and foreign secretaries together created health programs for women in India and mass literacy programs for villagers in China. They sponsored student conferences on a beach in Uruguay and in Fort Hare in South Africa. They spread physical training and physical education across the continents.

But secretaries learned as well as taught, and in two generations they began to describe their work as "world service" rather than "foreign work." Foreign secretaries became fraternal secretaries. Local Christian leaders asked missionaries and fraternal secretaries alike to see themselves in work that was multilateral, rather than unilateral.

It is not enough for one nation to bring another nation a gift, said one Chinese leader. Rather, "prophets and seers" should go from nation to nation, "interpreting and sharing with each other the best that is in our life until together we have built up in this world the fullness of life which God intends for us to have and enjoy."

James Phelps Stokes, New York philanthropist and YMCA leader who financed association buildings in Paris, Rome, and the one in St. Petersburg.

The St. Petersburg association under construction.

A Bible class at St. Petersburg.

The St. Petersburg association served young men from the lower middle class.

The shower baths at St. Petersburg.

Madras, India.

The Panama Canal Zone.

Blois, France.

Local Centers of
Christian Affection

Cairo (Central Branch).

Riga, Latvia.

Fort Hare, South Africa. In this
building, Max Yergan held the first
interracial student conference.

Laying the cornerstone of the association building in Hong Kong, February 10, 1917.

The association building in Shanghai, China, 1925

The Laying of the Cornerstone
Jerusalem Y.M.C.A.
July 23, 1928.

Professor C. H. Robertson giving his
famous gyroscope lecture, recounted in
John Hersey's novel, *The Call*.

Officials of Fukien Province in China at a special science lecture presented by Professor Robertson in connection with evangelistic meetings there in October 1914. The governor of the province is in the front row at center right. The general is in the front row center left.

衛生能生利
HEALTH PAYS DIVIDENDS

William Wesley Peter, who went to China as a medical missionary, headed the health division of the National Committee of China Young Men's Christian Associations.

Two figures used in Dr. Peter's public health campaigns, Cadaverous Mr. Cholera and Happy Mr. Health. They insisted on marching in daily parades in the health campaign.

為紀念躍躋人湘魯醫展衛生偉陸開會借用湘南省教育會開會各育教督基

A lecture audience on ladies' day in the public health campaign at Changsha, 1915.

A poster hall and exhibition area set up for a public health campaign.

The staff of the visual education laboratory in Shanghai, 1914. Standing at the right is David Z. T. Yui, a graduate of Harvard who became general secretary of the China associations in 1916. Professor Robertson is seated at the right.

Y. C. James Yen, who developed a mass literacy program for Chinese laborers in France during World War I. When he returned to China after the war, the YMCA sponsored his literacy work there.

Chinese laborers on a boat on their way to France.

In France the YMCA established 140 huts staffed by 109 secretaries for the Chinese. Here a group is leaving a hut in northern France after a lecture.

Chinese laborers celebrating Chinese Festival Day, on the fifteenth day of the eighth moon.

Sherwood Eddy Comes Home

Sherwood Eddy was twice converted. His first conversion occurred, he said, in his early adolescence, when the "Christian message came to me as a simple personal experience." Some years later, when he was studying at Yale University, he began to see that his satisfying personal religion was selfish. He started to search for ways to share it with others.

Eddy graduated from Yale and studied at Union and Princeton theological seminaries. When his father died in 1894, he inherited a comfortable sum. In 1896, then, he sailed for India to try to share God's word with other people. He spent his next 19 years in foreign work and world service.

Eddy made a speech at the 1928 convention of the Student Volunteer Movement for Foreign Missions. It was called "Can We Still Believe in Foreign Missions?" In it,

Eddy recalled some changes caused by the First World War, as devout Christians watched enlightened nations slaughter their young. Some beliefs changed—or shattered. Many people turned from a theology of individuals to one concerned more with the world in which individuals lived. In the aftermath of the war, Eddy had his second conversion. "I saw the War," he said, "as only a symptom of the striving world beneath. I

The site of Sherwood Eddy's first lecture in the Forbidden City, 1914. The meeting place was a special mat-shed erected close to the altar where the emperor formerly worshipped the spirits of the land. A half-holiday was granted to students who wished to attend his lecture.

saw the world rent and divided in industrial, racial and international strife—a world of sordid material-ism, autocratic exploitation and organized militarism, over prepar-ing for further war.

"Now there broke upon me," he said, "the first gleams of a social gospel that sought not only to save individuals for the future, but here and now in this world of bitter need, to Christianize the whole of life and all its relationships—

industrial, social, racial, interna-tional. Religion was not primarily something to be believed, or felt; it was something to be done, a life to be lived, a principle and a program to be incarnated in character and built into a social order. This social gospel added a new dimension to life; it raised it to a higher power. As I had once seen Christ identi-fied with the need of distant pagan lands, I saw Him now, hungry and athirst, naked, sick and in prison,

in the pagan practices and the blighted lives of our social order both at home and abroad."

Can we still believe in foreign missions? Yes, Eddy answered, but only if we served at home in the United States as well as abroad.

[from Gordon Poteat (ed.). *Students and the Future of Christian Mis-sions*. New York, Student Volunteer Movement for Foreign Missions, 1928. pp. 75-93.]

The central student YMCA in Manila, the Philippines, after and before.

Chapter **10**

Some Other Casualties of War

Casualties of war are usually marked by body counts. Rarely would we add an individual building to such a list. Yet seeing these "local centers of Christian affection" in ruins reminds us that we are part of a world movement. Damage to one is damage to all.

Wars, police actions, and regional conflicts yield other casualties as well: the soldiers in prisoner-of-war camps, Japanese-Americans sent to internment camps, orphans and "unaccompanied" children, refugees from fratricide and genocide. These displaced persons likewise remind us that we are citizens of one world served by Young Men's Christian Associations.

Berlin.

Some wrecked
"local centers of
Christian affection."

Warsaw.

Kobe, Japan.

Nanking, China.

Russian prisoners of war in a German camp, 1919.

Russian and Polish soldiers in Minsk, Russia, outside the YMCA hut.

Czech prisoners of war in a Russian camp in Siberia. They are at work in a shoemaker's shop started by the YMCA.

[...] army soldiers imprisoned by Germany in what the record calls East Russia, 1920.

Prisoners of war entering a camp in Germany in World War II.

American prisoners of war sleeping in a German camp.

Orphans from Armenia who have just
been given emergency clothing by the
YMCA and the Near East Relief
representatives.

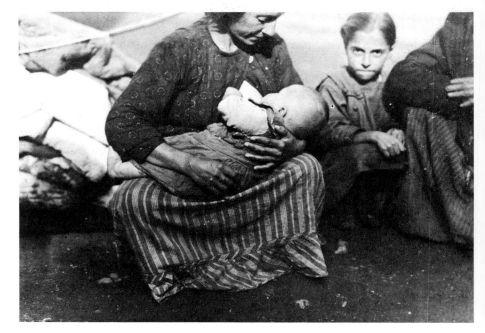

A mother and her children living on
the sidewalks of Thessalonika, Greece,
1922. "Two or three months of this sort
of life will kill masses and unfit those
who survive for civilization."

A group of refugees sent to camp in Thessalonika, with funds raised by friends and YMCA workers. Average weight gain in two weeks at the camp was three pounds.

Russian orphans picnic at Camp Mayak at Florida-on-the-Marmara Sea, 1922.

Japanese-Americans interned at a government camp in California, March 23, 1942. The YMCA served these and other detainees.

"Estonian YMCA members in a displaced persons camp at Geislingen, Germany, about to partake of their first communion under the leadership of their own pastors, also displaced persons in the U.S. zone."

Halyna Knysz, child center leader, and two Ukrainian children in a displaced persons camp served by the YMCAs.

Jan Malecki, a nine-year-old Polish
war orphan, at a YMCA home for
displaced children.

John R. Mott with the board of directors of the Nagasaki Young Men's Christian Association some time before the second world war.

John Raleigh Mott

At age 20, John R. Mott was one of the 100 students at Mount Hermon who pledged themselves to missionary work, "this great work of giving all men an opportunity to know Christ."

John R. Mott lived his next 60 years in Christian service, not as a missionary to other lands but as a builder and executive of the YMCA, the Student Volunteer Movement for Foreign Missions, the World's Student Christian Federation, and many—so many—other international and religious organizations.

Life interrupts our plans, even those made by a person of John R. Mott's singular determination. His devotion to making the abstract ideal of the brotherhood of man concrete was interrupted by two world wars and other local, but still lethal, conflicts. He responded by leading YMCA prisoner-of-war work during both world wars and helping displaced persons.

John R. Mott was awarded the Nobel Peace Prize in 1946 because, the Nobel Prize Committee said, he was "true to the call which he as a young student heard." He was not the missionary he imagined that day at Mount Hermon, but he remained "indefatigable in the service of Christ" and the ideal of the brotherhood of man.

Chapter 11

Growing Up Trying to Avoid Absurd

This is a chapter about innocence and earnestness, about a generation of adolescents who grew up shielded from the horrors of depression and war that their parents had just witnessed. They worked hard to avoid being square, but being "beat" was much worse. Beatniks, who didn't want to earn an honest living, were as perplexing as they were unsettling. How could people not care?

There were teams. All the boys and even a few of the girls were on teams. There were also student government and model legislatures, and places to prepare for the serious adult world ahead.

In retrospect, it seems the calm before the storm of the 1960s and what came after that. Square or not, it was good to be there.

At an exhibit, October 1957.

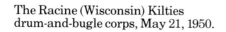

The Racine (Wisconsin) Kilties
drum-and-bugle corps, May 21, 1950.

The beagle competition at the YMCA
in Carney's Point, New Jersey, 1947.

Craft work at the nature cabin at
YMCA Camp Ockanickon, Medford,
New Jersey.

Officers of the Junior Hi-Y at Findlay, Ohio.

Baseball Hall of Fame members Jackie Robinson (kneeling) and Roy Campanella (standing) with members of the Jackie Robinson Club at the Harlem Y. Before his baseball career, Robinson starred in four sports at UCLA.

These members of the YMCA women's volleyball team of Dallas competed in the national volleyball tournament at Memphis, May 1957.

Members of the 1953 YMCA national basketball championship team from the Christian Street YMCA in Philadelphia. The man among men holding the ball is 16-year-old Wilt Chamberlain.

The Atlanta City YMCA produced these South Jersey champs in the 115-pound class.

The 1964 championship baseball team in the Ed Charles Downtown YMCA League in Kansas City, Missouri.

Teenage canteen entertainers, August 1946.

Bopping at the jukebox at the YMCA
in Ridgewood, New Jersey, 1963.

Concentrating at a Youth and Government session.

Passing the light at a moving-up ceremony for freshman-sophomore Tri-Hi-Y members at the railroad YMCA in Florence, South Carolina, 1957.

The Eternal Question

Women, historian Howard Hopkins observed, have been the "movement's eternal question mark." Should we admit them? If we admit them, should they be counted for purposes of representation? If we hire them, should we give them the title "secretary?" What if local associations persist in providing services for them?

Leaders debated the questions. Cephas Brainerd, chairman of the International Committee, and Robert Ross McBurney, leader of the New York association, were among the early leaders who believed that the YMCA would succeed only if it focused on work for young men, by young men. Their opinions echoed established nineteenth-century wisdom that rigidly separated men and women into public and domestic spheres; they also foreshadowed contemporary market research.

Other leaders differed. The Reverend Thane Miller of Cincinnati, who carried his Bible and was no respecter of conventional wisdom, reminded his fellows that men were not meant to live alone. More bluntly, Dwight Moody threatened to go on the "warpath with his tomahawk" against those who would exclude women.

Formation of the first Young Women's Christian Associations in the 1860s eased the pressure to admit women. Local associations persisted, nevertheless, in admitting women and girls, at first through the side door of women's auxiliaries. Eventually there were gym privileges one afternoon a week and an occasional Bible class. Ellen Brown became a boys work secretary—the first—at Buffalo. Tri-Hi-Ys blossomed.

In the twentieth century, women won the right to vote. More of them worked outside the home. Fears that educating women would wither their reproductive organs came to seem foolish. Within the YMCA and throughout society, the walls that had kept men and women in their separate spheres tumbled down.

Membership of women and girls grew. Constitutions and membership procedures changed. More and more young women, including those in the photo to the left, came to stand in the tradition of Annie Wittenmyer, Ellen Brown, Gertrude Ely, and Addie Hunton. One hopes Dwight Moody can see them now.

Trident awards to "Y Whizzes" at the Anaheim (California) YMCA, 1962.

The Hoffman family in the YMCA/Monsanto Family Run to the Arch, St. Louis, 1983.

Chapter **12**

The Joy of Inclusion

In August 1987, Solon Cousins, national executive director, wrote to Young Men's Christian Associations in the United States, inviting them to contribute photographs for the final chapter of this history. He specified only that the photographs document work after 1960 and that they be identified and dated if possible.

In response to his request, 137 associations sent more than 2,000 photographs. The following images are representative of the 2,000. They testify eloquently to what is of value to Young Men's Christian Associations today.

Water exercise class for seniors at
St. Louis, 1987.

The YMCA of Kauai hosting the
YMCA of Osaka, Japan, at the first
international family camp program at
Camp Naue, July 1987.

Ghana YMCA volunteers meet with
Birmingham, Alabama, visitors.

Dominoes players in the lobby of the "old" YMCA at Ashland, Kentucky, 1961.

Breaking ground for a new building of the YMCA of Greater New York.

Friends at Centerville Mills Camp of the Cleveland YMCA 1961

South Berkeley (California) YMCA, 1981.

Part of the Tri-Gra-Y program for girls at Sioux Falls, South Dakota, 1974.

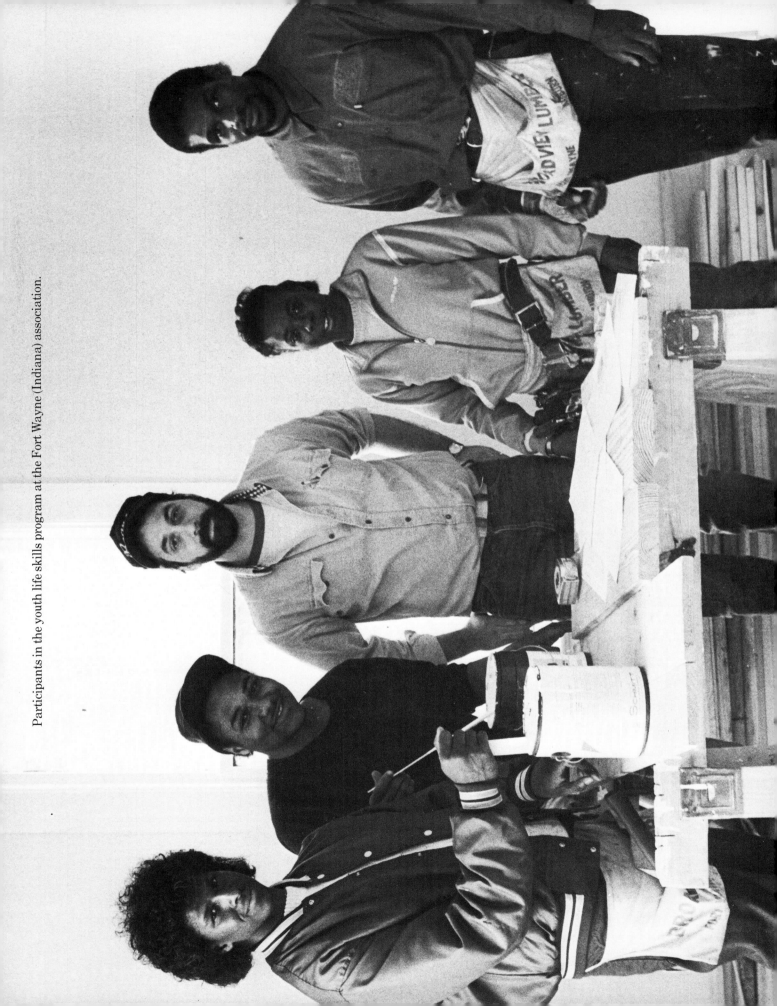

Participants in the youth life skills program at the Fort Wayne (Indiana) association.

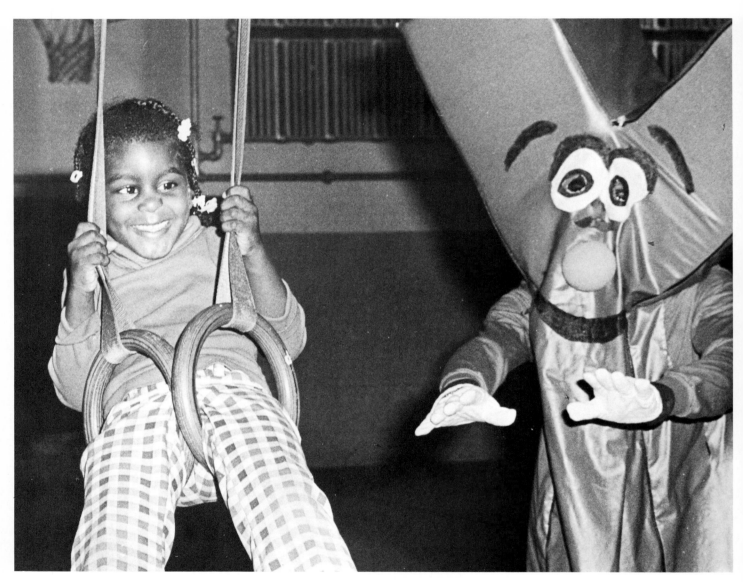

"Squeaky Sneakers" with "The Y Guy" at the Niagara Falls (New York) association's preschool program, 1982.

Wendy Ikezaki of the Nuuanu Branch of the Honolulu Y receiving a distinguished Youth Service Award from President Bill Aull, March 1971.

A youth basketball coach with two of her children who are team members in Hollywood, California.

An aquatics instructor at Scottsbluff, Nebraska, hugging a disabled child, 1986.

Two participants in the Sunbury, Pennsylvania, foster grandparent program, 1985.

The annual family pumpkin hunt at Waukesha, Wisconsin, October 1980.

Counselors with campers at Camp
Erdman, Honolulu, July 1980.

Batting practice at Ridgewood, New
Jersey, 1980.

Bob Elliott, former basketball star at
the University of Arizona, at free-
throw practice with a friend in
Tucson, 1986.

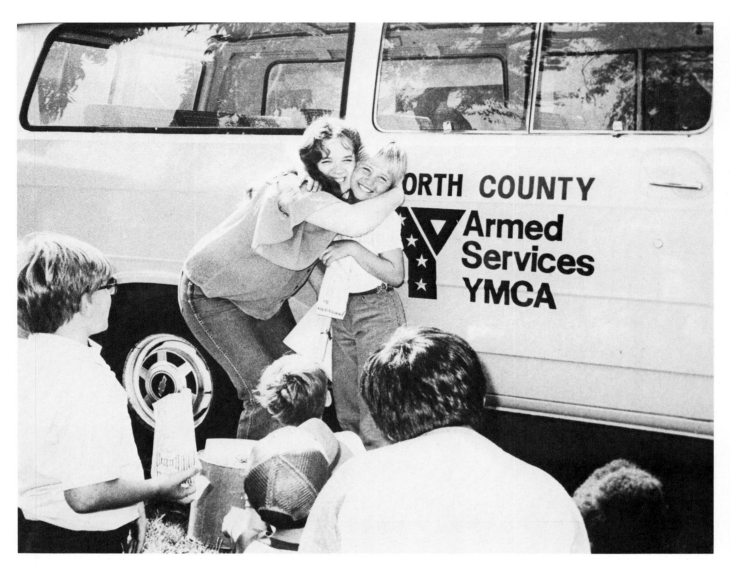

An armed services Y worker in
front of the fun bus in Oceanside,
California.

On the grass at Meadow Day Camp at the Oak Park association in Illinois.

Family camp at the YMCA Lake of the Ozarks branch of the St. Louis association, 1981.

Joy in the water at the Oshkosh
(Wisconsin) YMCA, May Day, 1986.

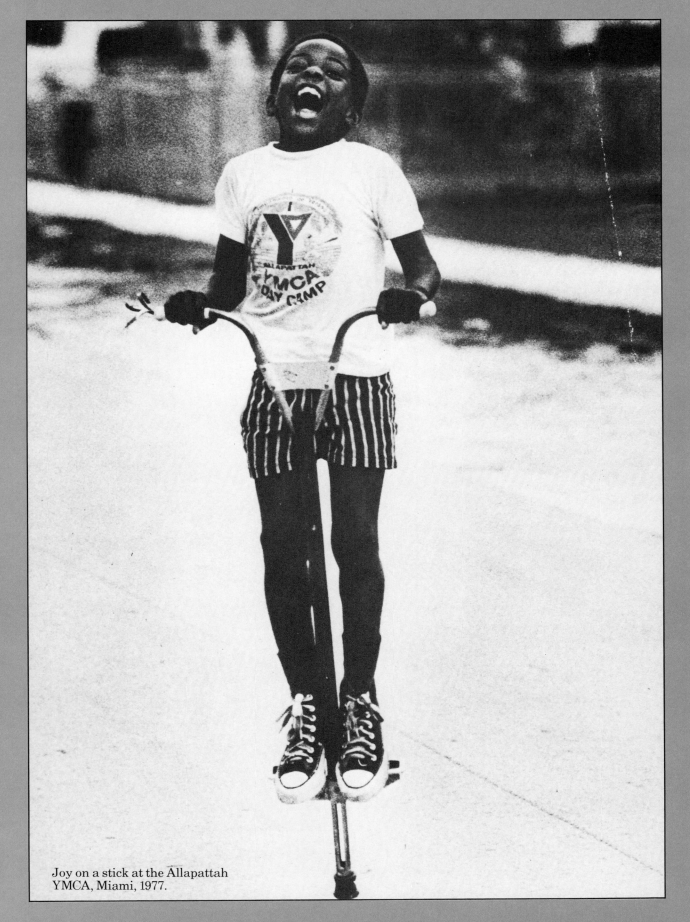

Joy on a stick at the Allapattah
YMCA, Miami, 1977.

An Indian princess at Mason City, Iowa, 1976.

A toddler at the child care center in Manchester, New Hampshire, 1987.

Thoughtful participant at the Los Angeles YMCA.

Summer program at Daytona Beach, Florida, 1985.

A happy day camper at Akron, Ohio.

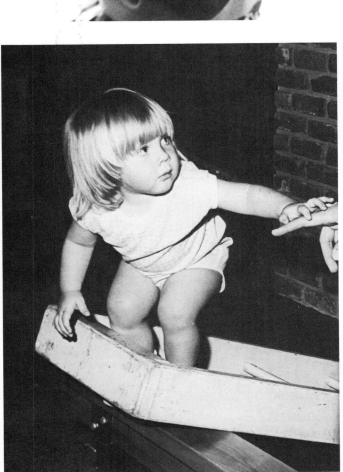

You & Me, Baby class at Tucson, 1987.

A senior working out in Baltimore, 1985.

A junior resting after working out at
Daytona Beach, Florida, 1975.

At the terminal in Philadelphia, 1986.

Broadcasting from the West County branch of the St. Louis YMCA, 1986.

Chef takes a break, 1963.

Climbing the chimney of Frost Valley's Hayden Lodge in Oliverea, New York, 1975.

Strength training at Kankakee, Illinois, 1979.

Working out at Lincoln-Belmont
Branch, Chicago.

Harold Davis in the glow of the
triangle at the National Council
meeting, May 1983.

Coretta Scott King kicking off the
capital campaign in Minneapolis,
1973.

Members of the YMCA of Scottsbluff, Nebraska, wave good-bye and hello.

Chronology of Events

Including a number of the
most-asked-about dates and events.

1844 George Williams and 11 other young men organized first Young Men's Christian Association, London, England, June 6.

1851 First YMCAs in North America organized, Montreal and Boston.

1853 First association for colored men founded by Anthony Bowen, a freed slave, District of Columbia.

1854 First national meeting of YMCAs, organized by William Chauncy Langdon, in Buffalo, New York. Delegates agreed to form a voluntary Confederation of YMCAs of the U.S. and British Provinces (Canada).

1855 World's Alliance of YMCAs formed at world conference in France, adopted Paris Basis as mission: to unite young men who have accepted Jesus Christ as God and Savior and who wish to be His disciples in faith and life and extend His Kingdom amongst young men. Differences of opinion on other subjects, however important, shall not interfere.

1856 First student associations formed at Cumberland University, Lebanon, Tennessee, and Milton Academy, Milton, Wisconsin.

1857 New York City YMCA offered classes in gymnastics.

1859 First YMCA building constructed, Baltimore.

1861 YMCAs formed United States Christian Commission for troops' temporal and spiritual comfort in Civil War; 5,000 volunteers worked at battlefields, hospitals, camps, prisoner-of-war compounds. First Armed Services YMCA work.

Robert Ross McBurney hired as general secretary of the New York City YMCA, the single most influential YMCA of the nineteenth century.

1863 Meeting in Chicago, Northern YMCAs dissolved national confederation.

1864 Chicago convention of North American YMCAs created Executive Committee of YMCAs of the United States and British Provinces (Canada) as formal national body.

1866 Executive Committee located in New York City.

A layman, William Earl Dodge, Jr., added "physical" to the New York City YMCA mission statement, creating the widely copied fourfold purpose: "the improvement of the spiritual, mental, social, and physical condition of young men."

1867 First YMCA building with its own gymnasium opened in Chicago and three months later burned to the ground.

1868 Executive Committee hired its first full-time national employee, Robert Weidensall, to organize YMCAs along the Union Pacific Railroad lines. He later organized rural and student YMCAs.

First State YMCA established, Connecticut.

1869 First boys work department organized, Salem, Massachusetts.

Richard Morse hired by Executive Committee to edit *Association Monthly* magazine.

First colored student YMCA formed at Howard University, Washington, D.C.

National convention adopted "Portland Basis," limiting those at future conventions, and by implication all YMCA boards and membership, to male members of Protestant evangelical churches.

1871 First state secretary appointed, Samuel Taggart of Pennsylvania.

Association of General Secretaries formed, later called Association of Professional Directors.

1872 Railroad YMCA first established at Cleveland passenger station.

Richard Morse named general secretary of Executive Committee, a post he would hold until 1915.

1873 First permanent rural work established, Illinois.

1874 National Association of German YMCAs established.

1877 Intercollegiate student work began. Luther Wishard named first national student work secretary.

1879 First permanent Army association established, Fort Snelling, St. Paul, Minnesota.

First Sioux Indian YMCAs reported, Dakota Territory. Organized by Thomas Wakeman, son of Chief Little Crow.

Henry Brown hired as national secretary to promote association work among colored men.

Executive Committee renamed International Committee, reflecting United States and Canadian support.

1881 Robert Roberts hired by Boston YMCA. He would coin word *bodybuilding* and develop exercise classes that anticipated today's fitness workouts.

1882 Association work begun among miners and lumbermen, Pennsylvania and Wisconsin.

1883 YMCA national office formally incorporated as the International Committee of the Young Men's Christian Associations of the United States and Canada.

1884 First summer training institute for YMCA secretaries, Lake Geneva, Wisconsin.

1885 Jacob Bowne donated his YMCA archives to the International Committee.

Sumner Dudley established first residential summer camp for boys, Orange Lake, near Newburgh, New York.

Work among Indian (native American) students organized at Santee Normal Training School, Santee, Nebraska.

YMCA's first indoor pool, called a swimming bath, Brooklyn, New York.

School for Christian Workers opened at Springfield, Massachusetts. It included a YMCA department which quickly became its major emphasis. In 1890 it became the International YMCA Training School, and later Springfield College.

1886 Ellen Brown hired as first boys work secretary, Buffalo, New York.

Bible school at Mount Hermon boys school, near the Dwight Moody summer home in Northfield, Massachusetts, drew about 250 students, mostly from YMCAs at almost 100 colleges. Student missionary uprising began as 100 signed up to evangelize the world in a generation.

1888 William Hunton became first black general secretary of an association, Norfolk, Virginia.

1889 Annual convention approved foreign work (later called World Service). Two secretaries appointed: Jonathan Swift, Japan, and David McConaughy, India. More than 700 would follow.

First high school YMCA, later known as Hi-Y, Chapman, Kansas.

Luther Gulick, Springfield College physical director, proposed triangle for YMCAs as symbol of unity of Christian personality: body, mind, spirit.

1890 Colored men's department created with William Hunton first national secretary.

YMCA Institute and Training school, later George Williams College, founded campuses at Chicago and Lake Geneva, Wisconsin. Chicago campus closed 1986.

1891 James Naismith, working for Luther Gulick at Springfield College, invented basketball.

1892 Education work department organized, with George Hodge hired as first national secretary.

1894 Queen Victoria knighted George Williams on the occasion of the 50th anniversary of the YMCA's founding.

1895 Physician Charles Eastman became first national secretary for Indian work.

W. G. Morgan invented volleyball, Holyoke YMCA, Massachusetts.

John R. Mott founded World's Student Christian Federation.

First Navy association organized, Brooklyn, New York.

1900 Building boom began, 290 put up in 16 years, with pools, gyms, residences, meeting rooms, game rooms, libraries.

1901 YMCAs in North America celebrated their 50th anniversary in Boston.

Edgar Robinson named first boys work national secretary.

1905 Sir George Williams died in London, buried in St. Paul's Cathedral.

1906 Water safety and learn-to-swim campaigns launched. George Corsan, Toronto, hired by Detroit YMCA, revolutionized teaching with mass swimming lessons, dry land drills, the crawl.

1907 YMCA Press (later Association Press) established.

1909 Father-and-son movement began, Providence, Rhode Island.

1910 Chicago philanthropist Julius Rosenwald offered $25,000 to any city that could raise $75,000 for a building for YMCA work with Negroes. A dozen were built in the following decade.

1912 Canadian associations formed their own national organization.

Conference on the Association Profession organized as a caucus of secretaries to create an agenda for the national organization and as a force for change.

1915 John R. Mott became the second national general secretary of the International Committee.

1917 The day the United States entered World War I, John R. Mott pledged YMCA support for soldiers to President Woodrow Wilson. Eventually 26,000 men and women served in YMCA canteens at home and abroad.

YMCA appointed a National War Work Council. From it grew a coordinated campaign for contributions with six other charitable agencies serving the soldiers, raising $200 million and advancing the idea of federated fund drives.

1919 Interracial commission (later Southern Regional Council) set up in Atlanta by W. D. Weatherford, a YMCA executive and founder of the Blue Ridge Assembly, in North Carolina.

1920 YMCA Army Education Commission awarded 10,000 scholarships to war veterans for YMCA schools and colleges.

Y's Men's Club organized, Toledo, Ohio.

1922 With the advent of the Retirement Fund, a group of secretaries formed the International Association of Retired Secretaries, later IARD, when the title secretary gave way to director.

1923 Constitutional convention in Cleveland set up two bodies, the General Board (later renamed the National Board) and the National Council. YMCA purpose was set at bringing the "young manhood and boyhood" of the United States and other lands "under the sway of [God's] kingdom."

1926 Harold J. Keltner, St. Louis YMCA, and Joe Friday, an Ojibway, began Y-Indian Guides parent-child programs based on the Indian family model.

1929 Onset of Great Depression forced National Board to make major budget reductions through the 1930s: foreign work curtailed, administrative emphasis shifted from state to multi-state areas.

1931 Cleveland national convention adopted revised statement of purpose that formally eliminated theological tests of membership, including the historic Portland Basis of 1869. It identified the YMCA as "a world-wide fellowship of men and boys united by a common loyalty to Jesus Christ for the purpose of building Christian personality and a Christian society."

1933 The Association of Secretaries formally recognized and admitted women secretaries.

1936 First Youth and Government program of citizenship and leadership training, State YMCA of New York, Albany.

1939 National Council began its support of the World Alliance program for War Prisoner Aid. It served nearly 6 million prisoners of war in over 30 countries during World War II.

1941 YMCA and five other national organizations serving the military formed United Service Organizations (USO) to manage work with armed forces in World War II.

1945 Following World War II, YMCA continued relief work in Europe: repatriation, resettlement, other programs for refugees and displaced persons.

1946 Nobel Peace Prize awarded jointly to John R. Mott and Emily Greene Balch.

1951 Centennial of the YMCA in the United States celebrated under the banner, "Faith for the Future" in a convention largely made up of young people and lay leaders.

Compiled by
 Kendal Lyon
 Dagmar Getz
 David Carmichael

National Volunteer Leaders

U.S. YMCA NATIONAL VOLUNTEER (LAY) LEADERS

1867-1892	Cephas Brainerd
1892-1894	Elbert B. Monroe
1895-1910	Lucien C. Warner
1910-1923	Alfred E. Marling

──────1924 Constitution──────

National Board Chair

1923-24	James M. Speers
1925	Fred W. Ramsey
1926-33	Adrian Lyon
1934-39	William E. Speers
1940-43	W. Spencer Robertson
1944-46	Ralph W. Harbison
1947-48	James C. Donnell, II
1949-50	Harper Sibley
1951-54	Eugene R. McCarthy
1955-60	Vivian C. McCollom
1961-66	J. Clinton Hawkins
1967-69	Wilbur M. McFeely
1970-72	Richard C. Kautz
1973-75	E. Stanley Enlund
1976-77	William E. Schneider
1978-80	Elija M. Hicks, Jr.
1981-83	Dale A. Vonderau

National Council President

1924	Adrian Lyon
1925-26	Fred W. Ramsey
1927-28	David W. Teachout
1929	W. Spencer Robertson
1930-31	Francis S. Harmon
1932-33	George B. Cutten
1934-35	Frederick W. Smith
1936	Beatty B. Williams
1937-39	Eskil C. Carlson
1940-41	Ralph W. Harbison
1942-43	Frank S. Bayley
1944-46	Howard A. Coffin
1947-48	Kirtley F. Mather
1949-50	Eugene R. McCarthy
1951-52	Harper Sibley
1953-54	William J. Grede
1955-56	James C. Donnell, II
1957-58	Clifford C. Gregg
1959-60	J. Clinton Hawkins
1961-62	Herbert E. Evans
1963-64	Beach Vasey
1965-66	W. Walter Williams
1967-68	George Gullen, Jr.
1969-70	Frank E. Masland, III
1971-73	Donald M. Payne
1973-75	Belford V. Lawson
1975-77	Ralph S. Mason
1977-79	James R. Bellatti
1980-81	James O. Plinton
1982-83	Egie Huff
1983-84	Harold Davis

──────1984 Constitution──────

National Board Chair

1983-85	L. Stanton Williams
1985-87	James W. Ashley
1987-	Sam Evans

National Professional Leaders

U.S. YMCA NATIONAL PROFESSIONAL (EMPLOYED) LEADERS

1872-1915 Richard C. Morse, General Secretary	1954-1957 Jay A. Urice, General Secretary
1915-1928 John R. Mott, General Secretary	1957-1964 Herbert P. Lansdale, General Secretary
1928-1932 Fred W. Ramsey, General Secretary	1964-1971 James F. Bunting, General Secretary
1933-1940 John W. Manley, General Secretary	1971-1980 Robert W. Harlan, Executive Director
1941-1954 Eugene E. Barnett, General Secretary	1980- Solon B. Cousins, Executive Director

An aeroplane modeling class on the steps of the Rochester (New York) YMCA.

About the Author

Andrea Hinding was born and raised in St. Paul, Minnesota, where she graduated from Our Lady of Peace High School. After studying journalism for two years at Marquette University in Milwaukee, she transferred to the University of Minnesota. There she was awarded both a bachelor of arts and a master of arts in American history and now is a member of the faculty.

Hinding joined the university's staff in 1964 in the Social Welfare History Archives. From 1978 through 1984 she was the director of the Walter Library. In 1985 she became archivist for the YMCA historical collection, which is held at the university. She describes it as the best job in the world.

She is the author of a landmark women's reference work, the two-volume *Women's History Sources: A Guide to Archives and Manuscripts in the United States*. Hinding is past president and a fellow of the Society of American Archivists.

Members of the New York delegation to the 1865 YMCA convention at Philadelphia. Cephas Brainerd is seated at the center. Robert Ross McBurney is seated to the left. James Phelps Stokes is standing at the far left.